NEW AND SELECTED POEMS

Paul Sutherland was born in Ontario, Canada, in 1947, and arrived in the UK in 1973. He was the founder of *Dream Catcher*, an international literary journal, and his own writing has appeared in countless anthologies, newspapers and periodicals. He has produced ten collections of poetry since 1970, including *Journeying*, which was published by Valley Press in October 2012. He has an MA in English Literature from the University of York, and became both a Sufi Muslim (adopting the name Abdul Wadud) and a freelance writer in 2004. He lives with his wife in Lincolnshire.

New and Selected Poems

PAUL SUTHERLAND

Valley Press

First published in 2016 by Valley Press
Woodend, The Crescent, Scarborough, YO11 2PW
www.valleypressuk.com

ISBN 978-1-908853-77-6
Cat. no. VP0094

Copyright © Paul Sutherland 2016

A CIP record for this book is available from the British Library.

Cover photograph by Abigail Smith.
Text design by Rosa Campbell.

Supported using public funding by
ARTS COUNCIL
ENGLAND

LOTTERY FUNDED

Contents

Good reading & writing

To Malcolm

from Paul Sutherland

Louth
2021

To my granddaughters
Farrah Feather and Zulaykha Feather

May all warring families make peace
for the sake of their children

Grandfather and Grandmother

Émigrés 1913

Two bells. Young grandfather
stared from the Atlantic liner's prow
into transforming night.

He arrived boldly
with his still unmarried spouse.
And never once returned.

He left grandmother
in an entry port. She complained
to the moon till 'Papa' heard.

They travelled to a Scottish-named town
on Ontario's delicate shore
under a tree-columned slope.

For sixty years observed that view
and the same bed. Two stillborn sons
only my mum inherits.

Watch — familiar Julys
his model garden bruised by heroic light
the resistant iris above raccoon-threatened gold fish.

Listen to — frantic grandma
charging through the house, stripped-off
screaming 'Look, look at me.'

Their dying, three years apart;
twice mourners came to the same plaque
to watch old lives embark.

Muskoka Rescue

Deep asleep a mid-aged woman suddenly was awake.
'Most likely nothing' she thought in her lidded room
checking a clock's expression, 'perhaps an insomniac
loon ... breaking the water's peace... A natural thing...'
She grew more on edge, robing herself, stepped through
the cabin's screen-door. Her bare feet on the cool sand
she spotted a four year old shape wading into darkness.
Sprinted over the foreshore and plunged into shallows
erupting layers where pre-Columbian trees had fallen
and decomposed to make a silted floor. Grandma grabbed
that water-ringed shadow, shaking it awake, drew it back
to the shore. It seems that sleepwalking child was me.

Spring Jottings For Grandpa

I hope from his decaying
   interment, he retains
      a listening to absorb

how April quick voices
   undulate across
      fields, and a sighting

to detect under foot
   on dislodged stone
      a peacock butterfly

whilst over
   the rise comes
      quavering bleats

where small wings
   perch with a song
      on a surviving elm

and as if revered
   a curlew's lengthening cry
      draws a frontier

and some open gate's
   four-rung shadow leans
      against dry-stone wall

from where novice
   bees locate
      sweet-scented cups

and in a walled garden
   irises encased
      in purpled stems

and a stump, a relic
a besom wedge stands
by the threshold

where over the door is carved
Listen to the Earth
and it shall teach thee.

Grandpa's Day

Quiet-footed, suicide often creeps up on its victim.
To understand cause (Albert Camus once probed)
you need to sniff out more than the grand seizure.
Sliver of regret, hair-line mischance, a so brief half-
heard damning, least detectable nudge towards hope
anything can unhinge and trip someone into oblivion.
Quietly grandpa tripped into that same non-existence.
Not taking his life, but just past his eightieth birthday
with family engrossed round the leaf-lengthened table
he slipped out between the steaming roast and ice cream.
Among clacking of gathered china and noisy kitchen-talk
without a warning gasp, slumped in his padded chair.
Nearby, a grandson's *are you ok, Papa?* left in space.

Returning to My Homeland

At my grandparents' burial spot
where few had come to separate funerals
with many secrets sprinkled into the earth

I kneel, brush and polish.
In encroaching grass their shone floral design
reflects nothing of their past wishing.

I rise with stained knees and walk off...
with his and her terrors bonded to me while grey
travellers, Canada geese, stray among the plots.

Near-Death-Ness

My grand-birth-givers, male, female, might enquire
'Why didn't you stay; give us your candid years?

Now, we take up lodging in your imagination
but we can't confer on you what we could have

if you had stayed, kept striding through our home's
doorway, into the garden; much would have lasted

longer if you'd remained with us and not migrated
back to where we had come from decades in the past.

In return, flowers would have kept flourishing, if you'd
continued to nurse them each spring back into health.

We had a fortune for you to pick up from the veneer
table; black obsidians, dark blue sapphires you never

dreamed of if you'd endured the seasons of our ageing —
its love and onus of destiny, its courage and its fear.

You thought we had given you everything we could,
didn't realise that from our seams of near-death-ness

we'd more to unearth, to extract, gems we would have
revealed to your bewilderment — no need to jemmy a small

lock as you did when nine years of age. We imagine still
the peace you'd have bequeathed if you'd hugged our death-

beds and we would have passed on miracle over miracle.
Beside our burial site, the earth heaped, we would have

bestowed secrets that you must always fail to perceive
which cannot be handed on like clothes or books but

appear as vistas we still believe you could have occupied.
You did not come back. No response, to our call, to return'.

A Month Home
Some Time Ago

In the window seat, dozing; I dream I'm trekking through umbra of Fall trees, under Niagara Escarpment cliffs into a rocky basin. The temperature drops, light dying. I hear voices; see oranges and reds dancing in a stone ring encircled by adults and girls. I'm a hiker with a long ways to go but walk straight up to them. Someone speaks first, Come and join us, have some food. I feel their campfire's heat; my stomach rests. I tumble asleep. Suddenly, a small hand takes mine and places into my palm a stone. I read in flickering light, scratched on its surface, 'I want you to be my friend forever.'

Ladies and gentlemen
kindly fasten your seat-belts
we're beginning our descent.

Awake. I recall Granddad's and Grandma's Atlantic voyage, a year before The Great War. Today I have flown from Manchester England; hours later touched down in Toronto. At forty years of age, this arriving feels like a first home-coming. By birth-right with a Canadian passport I queue up at the customs' barrier, a stranger, almost without a country. Now after denials, I yearn to embrace new world origins. My aging father and mother greet me at Arrivals with non-stop hugging. We drive sixty kilometres to Hamilton in it looks like my dad's new limousine. I anticipate my visit to be more than affluent episodes, serial adventures despite their curative smiles. Homeward, on Highway 5, we speed past industrial acreage, strip malls, coffee take-outs, wasteland plots, and those big homesteads where three or four generations of vehicles honour a gravel driveway like medals gleaming on a veteran's chest. My home's September landscape opens before me revealed in its natural geography, the opposite of each of my fantasies. Our journey weaves between Lake Ontario's marshy-pocketed bays and the coloured slopes of the Niagara Escarpment; between fresh water and limestone, newness and history. Stepping out of the car, I hope sooner or later to be able to walk up and offer homage at my grandparents' grave.

September 18th

Westward, next door's stranger on his back veranda

glittering against
his craggy face — sun creeps
through foliage

It's hard to believe I have been here before. The notion of home seems a disguise for some other place as if a lifetime's sleight of hand. How can an original home exist? I can't see the intrinsic phenomenon that surrounds, my eyes won't submit; still in the UK, haven't caught up. After the excitement of arrival is absorbed and taste of an initial cup of tea fades, I'm half ashamed that I don't know the history or circumstance of the gentleman I'm gazing at. Does he know me? I look across back verandas, pass private boundaries. Is he asking 'who's this intruder who knows my neighbours? Does he know me?' I realise my acceptance, that this here and now is home, must happen slowly. The first 24 hours drift as smoke wisps towards received normality, submission to routine, dinner time, with lingering jet-lag dazing my sight.

September 19th

At home, the lights out...under the covers

estimating the hour
dad's clocks disrupt
stillness of sleep

September 20th

At my best friend's mother's house

crossing shade
nostalgia overwhelms
by sagging lilies

I owe much to the Black family. Can the poetic words above do justice to the love and support they've shown? A miniature must be read and re-read till a small house of 10 children on the side of a sacred marsh is portrayed. As a boy, I escaped to their sweet chaos, from my orderly home. Fled to a rash of lilies and the wildest *music of the spheres*, to an eccentric house on the very edge of a temperate jungle that later would be transformed to a black-top parking lot for the yet too near university. Mrs Black, a resourceful mother, found ways to bring charm and energy into her crowded home with lean corners of china statuettes. Each comic imaginable for her precocious sons was stacked by their bunk beds, *Flash Gordons* and *Batmans* among the rarer.

September 21st

At the 'Rock Gardens'

waterfall steps
mum and dad
conversing

green striking my face,
under, through, trying to find
childhood ways

No need for order: we children love to turn everything into chaos to understand it, to more truly live it. In naivety what's random becomes a manner of paradise. My 'no longer-young-ness' is reflected when I start to read and value labels, trying to store up each species' title, its associations and particularities, on each plaque a Latinised name under the common-place. Have I become too adult in my ways? The Rockery has grown over decades from a metamorphosed, deserted quarry.

September 22nd

Ruth at home

my sister hums —
bath-water gurgling
she prepares for work

When she's out of the house I
rummage the attic, a source
of distant mementoes, on shelves
in that triangular space under
the bird scratching shingles, on
blue-jean knees I discover in a box

ink-stained gold leaves,
letters to cremate...
whose past to purge?

September 23rd

At Webster's Falls
a favourite family beauty spot near
the city on the Niagara Escarpment's rim.
The current shepherded between
low well-pointed granite walls
with an arched viewing bridge
above the river. The unemployed
during the 1930s Depression undertook
such elegant constructing as part
of public works programmes. Grandfather
once palely coloured a picture of this cataract
c. 1914. I slid over ice-ripples above the falls,
c. 1960 my two sisters looking on in horror,
my brother debating if he should dare the same feat
whose key defensive quote was 'not often but wrong again'.

cascading
afternoon sparkles
in episodic leaps

September 24th

Family reunion at Grimsby Beach
on Lake Ontario: uncles, aunts and cousins
trade stories among nightfall's
scented pines. Church-going people:
in another age steamers docked
at the beach bringing Toronto pilgrims
to a park's tent tabernacle to worship.

Once angry at everyone, I belly-flopped
from the plank-less wharf and swam
to the next slump-shouldered pier
and wanted to stay out there —
hairless chest and swim-suit dripping —
no irritation on that half-submerged column.
I knew my rescuing cousin who
had won swimming competitions
was never far away: that summer's life-guard.

We sit on picnic benches around a barbeque
away from the Back 40, the swampy woods
where, as dad used to warn
us kids, the mosquitoes are 'big
enough to carry you away'.

musky fire —
bungalow of memories —
dives on blood

My three aunts

studded wedding
and keeper rings don't age
with crumpled hands

On the picnic table, their three sets of hands creased from labour, fruit-picking over long years, look joined, restful as if displayed in a downtown jewellery case. Close by, their husbands, my uncles, look on with their own outrageous feelings.

September 25th

In my brother's house

a 'Babar' for Elizabeth,
his daughter, my niece
(a cherished storybook
when mum read to me
in our upstairs apartment
when I was a wobbling toddler).

I give to a child —
why's your tail missing? — she asks
her soft tailored toy

For Elizabeth

She hasn't seen me for nine years since she was a baby I rock-a-byed in my arms. Now I inflict my love of literature on her innocence, nothing demanding; chase fairy tale words with an index finger in good faith, puzzling if she will keep up and if she, against expectations, will somehow remember me and that first far-distant cuddle.

have we bonded forever?
reading page after thin page
her turn then mine

In the evening...

*At Tulips with my young sister Ruth
and her best friend, Nancy both unmarried
and I'm expecting to be divorced anytime,
yet little is said to uproot the ritual of genteel
consuming in a round-table restaurant.*

in shorts, our waitress:
I object to her sleeve
in my cherry cake

September 26th

*At Niagara Falls.
My grandfather came here
in every season even if it meant
five or six punctures and tire patching
before arriving at the vast cataract's
uproar. Absent, that intrepid explorer.
Now we drive up and park more leisurely
paying five or six times over the odds
for a place to view the miracles.*

utterly joined
a rainbow-trio spans
the fiery gorge

as if waves
smashed — behind mist-clouds —
boulders

At the Horse Shoe Fall's edge

the world shutters
... looking for shelter
a dazed wasp

One of Mrs Black's adventurous boys, once, told, how for seconds,
  he saw
a white damsel, her shape-shifting in the torrent at the foot of that
  descent.

Crossing the Whirlpool Rapids

with starched ruffs
maddened currents churn
below our air-car

Who was the first to look down on this watery mayhem hoping to
keep peace between intimates? Honeymooners, soldiers, ex-partners
and sight-seers have stared and shared this suspended confined
space above nature's spectacle but yearned to alter their relationships,
to change someone's heart for the better.

Same day recalling the Welland Canal

When a youngster on a family Niagara trip, I demanded a detour to
the Welland Canal, to see its staircase climb the Escarpment. The
Flight Locks' entrance piers that began the ascent appeared
imperishable as twin ancient columns. A massive chain, intricate
and bold, great pools lifted by degrees over the landscape's face. I
longed to experience those rectangular voids, gleaming far down
with water, gripping sea-and-lake travelled ships. Before security
fences, in my shorts, (always in shorts until after a freak
thunderstorm one day going to school, soaked through, I was
allowed blue jeans) on dirty knees I'd crawl with a hunched
back to the lock's bevelled lip and stare down into green-blue
murky depths. Another sunk ocean-goer, with high masts and
flags, rose up towards my eye level, water pouring in through
the lock's upper doors, the lower ones fixed shut. 'The hugest
locks in the world', my dad would celebrate. Now I know there
was that Hoover Dam 1930ish grandeur tingling in me. The
audacious cargo ships climbed. But what did I gaze on,
kneeling, too afraid to stand upright and look so far below, my
mum and dad apparently certain I was safe at the brink? What
I stared into — was a glimpse of the Abyss, of something immense
and beyond control, but an engineering giant. Also at the
Niagara Cataract's edge, that sense of enormity conquered
smallness, my belief in me and my world. On every journey to
those Canadian-American Falls, from the back seat I'd protest
until the driver swerved toward the canal locks. No-one
understood my longing. I would read the historic plaque over again
and ask annoying questions. I tried to gain an insight into why
this phenomenon affected. I recall silence, a deep secret hush,
prevailing at the edge. Did I have to test fear; set courage
against wild depths again and again? I discovered in colossal
man-made chasms something that threatened existence,
that marked an end-point to what was for me believable;
yet it was ours species'. Nature's power and human construction
had meld in my mind to create a totality. No escape appeared
possible, if I slipped I knew, but, if I fell, it was…into what?

September 27th

Just older than me, my friend Walter has
made a home in the city down a humble street
after many removals, after attic squirrels had chased him
from my neighbourhood. He's a master at
cooking cabbage rolls: spreading the filling
and folding over the grey-green leaves to create
a delicious dish. He gazes from his tall back sash
perhaps recalling again how he once heard
on an unscrubbed tape his wife making love
with another man in his own front room
after he'd listened through the crackling
to his children's laughter.

fence-flowers
entangled with
shock-burdened years —

Walter and I visit a maternity ward.
We're strangers and now pretend
to be anticipating fathers waiting
to see our first off-springs in a cubicle.
No nurse asks us to leave or explain why
we've come to observe and there's
no admittance fee. Two images
coincide to create a proverb for birth:

as if a figurine
a sleeping lion
at an infant's
wrinkled feet

Aerial View

In his big Merc Walter drives
us over the Skyway Bridge -
(Walt eventually sold his prized car
after being stalked all day by a Merc-lover).
The bridge curves a masterpiece of span
and stress at the factory lined harbour —
Olympic flames from the steel mills' cauldrons
raw iron from the Minnesota ore fields.
The future may call it City of Waterfalls
but for many it will be Steel Town
with its hard hats and earned union dues
a history of labour unrest and lunch-pails
by slag contaminated crimson-worm water
which once shone limpid as any spring-fed lake.

a deep-draught *laker*
splits the bay without budging
fleets of cumulus

Alone, later that evening

Next door's new inhabitants won't be aware that their home was the site of my first passion. Falling for my neighbour's wife was stranger when she began to say yes. Did I have the courage to see through that desire and pain? Keep faith? I remember black swans were symbols of hoped-for children as if they could be ethereal creatures eluding stigma and blood. She was childless. Her solo foetus from her husband had been still-born. My loving hugs and kisses might have dissolved the grievance and grief. Iron comes from pristine veins, never affected. The heart requires fond refining to handle the source, the demands of forbidden love. All our industry is hapless against passion's potential for harm or healing; no surprise holy books disown its Phantoscope of emotions as lust.

a phantom-crazed house
I gawk at bay windows
scan its yearnings

Her house, parts of a vanished body, I'm drawn to a bedroom's bay
window, unaltered veranda and longing side profiles. Stare until its
architecture is erotic.

September 28th

My father in a photograph

I see you — shy one —
earthling — among elders
dropping your child-head

Hard to imagine my proud, forceful father as
reticent. A soldier, a plumber, a man who cleaned
the steel smelting furnaces sometimes, who stood up
to bosses and claimed he wouldn't be double-crossed.
Photograph albums mightn't lie and yet
looking through them, I'm exhausted until can do
nothing but gaze up at a tree. Family history without
enough research, snippets of another country,
unrefined feelings storm through me and yet
the most important moments might remain
un-imaged, un-recorded. Dad was kind also —
to us children when it was more necessary than
discipline, giving compassion which may've
had its birth-roots in incipient shyness

or in World War II battle scars
and grieving lost comrades.

powder blue mounted
some of nature's leaves
flicker without touching

old warrior's fingertips
tapping — my father
sits across from me

Dad sometimes communicates, a grin with a knowing glint in
green-brown eyes. Re-winds English wartime experiences, recalling
over and over, part a joke part serious, how publicans shouted,
'Time! Ladies and Gentlemen and Canadians.'

Nightfall drive to a home among orchards

Orchards in the Niagara Peninsula
are sacred sites of dad's boyhood
and still intact during my delinquent years
where too many cherries or peaches
made me happy and disgracefully sick...
coming home, sandy soil lodged between toes.
My farmer uncles swung low their heads
as they drove their snorting tractors under
the fruit loaded branches. Later most sold
their fragile labour intensive terra firma
for builders to erect new housing estates
or sub-divisions. The tension between
growth and construction is relived. Through
here too 1812 blue American soldiers crept
to discover a concealed resistant Canada.

chalice shapes
row by row ascend
with bowed limbs

To my godson, Scott, 20 years old
but looking back on his own innocence,
now he aspires to be a policeman
fighting crime in the province's capital.
I had charged against the walls
on my granddad-made rocking mare.
Did Scott do the same? I hadn't seen him
since he was an infant, then a toddler
now a young man ready to battle the world.

who conceived his
rocking horse that scarred —
riding to *bed-a-byes*?

September 29th

through grime
sentiments rage
in card-racks

By this point in my journey, my home-sojourn, feelings of hope and renewal are undermined by the frantic insistence that life goes on, and to mark any milestone we should be satisfied with greeting cards. But the window filth is too real to be seen through. I picture us all as mobsters even if idealism dies hard — and the stink's tactile — our feelings grow far too pained, too callous and convoluted for any cheerful cartoon characters and script to express them, to offer solace or congratulation. I'm breaking faith with wishy-washy commercialism with regret.

Walking thoughts

a teetering guide
humming on her 'lonesome' —
a child in her stroller

September 30th

Visiting my best friend, Don,
his wife Vanessa and children:
Selena, Aretha, Nicolas

A favourite lakeside woods,
the tensions in his marriage
below the fallen leaves,
but they put on a good front
for me and their children...

the woodlot another site
where the pristine fades
faster than the season.
We husk corn, and marvel
at harvest-fair winning pumpkins.
In the spring, they hunt
for piebald trilliums.

his family and I —
a rustling house
under flamboyant boots

At an old homestead

against a window pane
smear-marks
of a death-struggle

Don's father purchased this farm; it seems abandoned. My friend
and I feel like invaders or rescuers. The house with vast Victorian
dimensions suggests the ambitions of second and third generation
settlers or city dwellers wanting to return to the land, but altering
clayey soil to a market garden's loom is another matter. The circus
stunt nurtures a dream, to make the harsh terrain bloom.

To Selena, recalling Lucy in England

I've a god daughter,
your age, who long since
I can never hug

I suppose love of someone else's children is wasted feeling, yearning for bonds disdained. Yet reminders of caring persist, trembling my nerves like ridged shorelines from which the Lake's retreated to throw its froth at new shores.

October 1st

Don once hand-blew glass

Don Black teaches me to believe glass is never inert, never reaching the point of absolute compliance. Glass's countless reflections, colourations, are closer to its molecular truth than the fact you can pick it up, a transparent object, trusting its form won't melt away in your hands. Its fragility is an illusion against endless flow caught a second by the glass-blower. His artefacts used as functional pieces convey irony not lost on my best, long lasting friend from schoolhood days who wore black to celebrate or mourn, impossible to say which, and it still is.

Dust-matured crayons
rise from vases and bowls
of unchecked motion

Autumn wildflowers

Paradise's yellows
and purples crush
their peeling home

October 2nd

With mum and dad
visiting my grandparents' grave.

Pioneering immigrants
they arrived in Canada 1913
and were first to be buried. Few friends
left to come to their separate funerals.
So many hidden things gone to earth.
Once I saw my grandma scream
'look at me!' dressed only in her birthday-skin
with collapsed breasts and scarlet-traced eyes.
I sat in the living room listening to the stereo
with 'Papa'. Her command soared above
Wager's trumpet calls in the Ride of Valkyries.

Here they are presumed joined, underground.
I've seen my cabinet-maker grandpa weep
over his exquisite hand-shaped creations
in mahogany, oak, beech and walnut
over perfect tables and chairs, over chisel curls,
begging. He wanted to be a poet, wanted to
have a son that lived. Male scream
bound up against female scream... 'Just say
they've stepped out for three billion years'.

Once my grandma jabbed, 'if you're a poet
you know your grandfather isn't one.'

we kneel, rub
their bronze plaque —
the sun's reflected

travelling
between islands of mourners
in light waves

October 3rd

Home, in back room

'...careful there, Lorrie'
dad says, mum reaching
to water a plant

Dad believed that when he ditched his desire for alcohol (which had led him staggering home more than once or needing to be rescued from the rear seat of a taxi or from the gutter) that all quarrels with his wife, my mum, would cease — an endless truce would unfurl across their retirement like an undocumented dawn.

Mum, in a backroom armchair, reads the daily *Spectator* back to front. I enquire about this practice. She prefers to start with bearable local or incidental news, as sources and tributaries, before gradually with mounting awareness and withheld dread, she takes on the world news' headlines and the main story like an estuary.

October 4th

In the morning...

my work table bare
as if what I fear realised
till slipper steps pass

Of course I fear my birth-givers' demise, no matter how loved, with absence nothing will be the same. No feeling equals their kindness, if mostly expressed in passing. Their un-broken vows is something to marvel at; having not only stayed together but continue being 'lovey-dovey' before their children's eyes. They celebrate their home life with few interior doors as if all this was natural as falling off a slippery lakeshore log, (their bedroom was never closed to us).

Four hours we drive till we come
to my parents' cottage, near Buckhorn

what are nations and
their flags compared to these leaves
and countless needles?

through evergreens
what power roars
no star or colour —?

tree-outlined
the luminous gives back
one dark out-stretching

October 5th

'dear' mum says
'happy anniversary'
to rousing dad

44

I've seen enough of their wedding day, her white train to the floor, his dark suit, slim post war trauma smiles, to think I lived their moments in front of the flash.

her retching cough
from their room:
he's a light sleeper

Years of rising at 5 am has set an alarm clock ringing in his head for a pre-emptive waking. He can't bear to be late. Mum picked up her chronic cough when she visited me on a remote North Sea island — in August when weather was like December. The infection is blamed on me not her who sought the sublime, high altitude insular vistas of Shetland under the Arctic Circle.

After breakfast

steel guitar songs
seek my approval
from the petite kitchen

Afternoon

eddied currents...
rock-flows twinkle
with quartz

We stop by Adam and Eve Rocks: huge boulders dice-shape balanced on their ends, an arm's length apart; impossible not to imagine the two were placed by supernatural means, vestige of our first parenting. A geological sign of what intimate relationships might look like in their utopia. Far from the city, yet not that far, strangeness of the wilderness which is no wilderness begins to invade. The cottage, a human-fraction, a present moment against an ageless. The city's veil has been lifted and the bride is beyond anyone's imagination. Father, a retired plumber and his wife, retiring knitting-needles, find meaning in nation-less trees, rock and water. In later years, dad has exposed a love of ballet and a dread of mashed potatoes. Like all he's an individual, not a type-cast worker.

dad stills the motor,
mum jumps out to snap
lengths of autumn

a bowed audience
white-armed birch along
the farthest beach

Late afternoon, back at the cottage
(with its two roof levels surrounded by spruce)

golds
from a balcony's view
crinkle in pools

so, so oblique
the moon's earliest arc
from blue

Evening meditation

a curving sky,
eyes shut, I realign stars
from my bedroom

October 6th

constellations
over a looking glass
the woods awestruck

a promised shower
from quietest night
drips through dawn

out in the car,
classical music we drive
by enflamed tree-hedges

October 7th

Jill

Years ago, a twelve year old girl etched her name and address on
a page of slate asking me to be her friend. I was twenty two. She
ended each correspondence with, 'hopefully forever'. We exchanged,
over two and half years, four or five letters. Her mum and dad
objected and a schoolmate claimed my attention was misunderstood.
I tried to offer what Jill had asked by stone, then later with pleas on
birch bark, like a Native American, as if her request was without
pretentions, without anything to fear. Loneliness perhaps made
her courageous and trusting. My disappointments helped me
accept her teenage affections. A tricky mix between male and female.
She was a Swedenborgian, chanting free religious songs around

the campfire by the Niagara Escarpment when I first met her one evening under its rocky cliffs — a girl-inheritor of that mystic's psychic tradition.

I re-read her chosen words in letters and valentines, her brave gangling script, thick and uneven inside Christmas cards, descriptions of what she was doing at school, wanted to become, her private likes, beautiful things she wanted to share with me and her fierce fierce dislikes. Her wishing sounds so uncomplicated on this grey-slate afternoon beyond street lights, I'm pained to think it unfulfilled. Left dangling, her words seem undervalued as this great land's esteem, beyond ownership or purchase price. Among scattered lakes and uninhabited isle-lets

I bed-in her stone
by cleft roots where
chipmunks 'churdle'

October 8th

On a solo walk

through taciturn
under-growing
coupled chickadees

rain-patters —
in bloom yellows —
wild snap-dragons

a spiral stairway...
scarlet leaves
ascend

At twilight. My shoes a little water-logged
trouser-cuffs muddy. Sneezing, a bit chilled
blowing my nose again. Pausing outside
trying to catch something more than the material
before we leave the cottage tomorrow...
long observing Sandy River's water...
no buzzing insects... something other than
nature and its unexplained elegance...thinking
about ancient masters on other shores... or
Matthew Arnold on Dover Beach

lost friendships
gemstones in wavelets
spiriting ashore

October 9th

We leave the cottage and drive towards North Bay

plummeting colours —
every mile startles —
lake sands and rock cheeks

At my sister Barbara's house with her husband Al,
and their boys, Neil, Jay and Graham

four year old street
I stroll without footpaths
to my sister's home

October 10th

In the morning

Tyrannosaurus —
and other dinosaur smiles
line my nephew's room

From a scenic lookout

melancholy
over-takes my gaze
across Lake Nipissing

My younger sister's early marriage, decades happy with three
off-spring, shows a route I could have taken if that route had been
open. It closed forever after my affair with my neighbour's wife —
a break in the proceedings that would force me out of my nation
and inaugurate a greater desire to write, dream and explore this

and other worlds. Are these real choices, perhaps not? But the melancholy on this day is pronounced enough for my sister with her elbow to nudge me from preoccupations. Her home resembles a toy shop flowing with colourful creatures gazing from each sofa's or armchair's corner with sawdust-filled smiles — this decor shocks my longing for the ascetic. Yet nearby Lake Nipissing appears more than stoical as if a missionary in pre-winter grey robes.

October 11th

Ruth arrives. Flurries on
Barb's front lawn; her husband
with a light-meter, trying
to catch the seminal moment
the unique split second
without caricature smiles

linking arms
in a boys' family
between two sisters

Ruth is single, I don't even know if
she has ever had a serious boyfriend —
but no doubt she's had dreams
of long shared happiness, no one can doubt that.
She now seems to be in my role, the first born
head of the family, she's stayed and I've migrated;
stayed on to look after failing mum and dad.

Leave-taking

accelerating...
I twist round to see
Isles of Manitou

Al, yesterday: 'to the first nations those islands were God's home',
pointing toward rock specks on the lake's horizon.

snow-slumbering
crimson trees
weighted with white

This freak Fall snow couldn't hold us for long, despite un-treated
roads and lure of cottage-life, soon we aim our hood back towards
the city's congested reality of skyscrapers and expressways. When
winter properly arrives, white lined tree branches will clash like
antlers and the fluffy ground glitter with rhinestones.

Returning south

reminiscence shines —
gingerbread fretwork
on Thanksgiving Day

summer time
when I came; maple reds
shout 'autumn'

black crowned white shields
mark highway 27
through glacial terrain

Roadside stall in southern Ontario

mammoth pumpkins —
orange deciduous above
white man's captured soil

Lost Nation

a horse
out of touch with earth
canters

Are we in contact with history, losses suffered by first nations of Canada, accepting evidence that we are aggressors, dictators, victims, escapees from European panics and politics, immigrant oppressors of another peoples' beliefs and aspirations? Not many years ahead Canada's existence would be tested by a vote, perhaps it was descendants of those early people who by inches saved confederation. I'm in touch with intimate history and can't raise one pledged name from that pre-settler past that knew this land. That chestnut horse canters, trots, a symbol, a totem, loosened but broken, its maverick spirit tamed. I hardly notice our compromise until home, my dad's exertions, mum's accommodating and each attempting to do their best for their returned, estranged first son.

October 12th

Home once more, in a spare hour again
I climb into the magician's cave of our attic
(some downstairs are displeased that I do).
Already the quest has become too diverse.
I'm among so much dust-veiled treasure,
era inside of era like a stack of bowls
from exotic styles, 50s, 60s, 70s, 80s.
Each dulled object sits out-moded,
abandoned to their fate
for a future age to puzzle
on the yesterdays left behind
finding a hint in museum-worthy junk
of what the past might have been
and yet was determined to throw away... though
no generation is in complete control.

pin-ups by hymn books
I search Papa's world
mum's long stored

The Old Neighbourhood

Evening walk through my primal neighbourhood
where the child-teen-man first strode and met his Sphinx...
heard accusations and praises and where he kicked
a pop can at a friend who'd pushed him too far
one night... the friend turned round bowed
at the assault. Something that doesn't always happen.

my provisos — old facades —
every street corner betrays
some first engagement

as if communing —
a hazy quarter
without influence

1968: we boys gathered under a street lamp, straddled our three
speed bikes, not wanting to get out of the saddle, to place our feet
on the concrete ground firmly felt too dangerous. We stared at
each other, mystified what being an adult might mean, what we
might have to stomach and ignore. We gazed off dumb-founded:
no chatter or girl-baiting or sports bragging, no poking, no
horsing around, no snacking. We seemed turned to granite for ages
the night Robert Kennedy was assassinated in front of our eye-balls
on TV screens, in each neighbourhood home, as if we might have
intercepted his murderer but somehow had failed to.

October 13th

Jackson Square Mall
in a coffee and donut bar

in enchanted shoes
many ensconced
nibble and escape

Return is not only about reconnecting, but meeting new strangers.
Some will become friends for a time or fantasies, others will pass
by — claim your heart and leave you free. They stay, unchallenged
by world vistas. Float around in claustrophobic malls looking for
something in mint condition, untarnished (I don't know what) or
seek its opposite. They pour over tropical location leaflets.

An old woman opening her compact

with her raincoat —
after dabbing cracked lips —
she begins to fight

I have seen my ancient aunts smear their lips — as if that one act redeemed every hoped-for event. Our need for cosmetics. I have been intrigued by cherry lips and indigo eye shadow, seduced to follow appearance, the effect of cheek-blush.

From adjoining clothes stores

in sync
to smoke and converse, at break
two salesgirls emerge

I hope my male gaze doesn't offend. They go about their ceremony as if used to being objects of an itinerant's attention. Working so long in a store might make a server feel available as an article of merchandise, and yet the gazer is left with a grey-screen of guilt. I can't see what I'm looking at; I know it, and they know it. A flick of ash and they disappear. This meditations on strangers leads to thoughts of long-lapsed friends. The twin conveyors of retail therapy keep aloof under the mall-roof shelter, perhaps not wanting to dampen their smoke signals.

Back to Walter

*Thinking about Walter's
lifetime of dissolutions*

with no repenting
a limestone quarry engulfs
his childhood home

For each one of us, the whole, not merely a local fragment, was different. Every rock-dig, wildflower, school bus and route across fields was other than it is now. The past we long for was someone else's present that they hardly appreciated when theirs. I'm longing for what others thought a disgrace...the bulldozed unknown. I grieve for my favourite fouled stream in a swamp-spotty valley of reptiles and tadpoles that became the route of Expressway 403. Where a farm stood, a log-house, then forest and a tread too soft for modern ears.

Tim Horton's

In the same coffee bar
famed for its cheap superb coffee
the place for a kangaroo court

the plaintiff...

an over-made-up face
with frightened spheres she sits down —
such hard-line eye brows

like jurors...

mall-drifters eavesdrop.
with a stabbing voice she recounts
a long injustice

October 14th

I saunter into the new Public Lending Library, no longer a 19th century stone mason's handiwork, pillared and corniced, ethos of a temple-cum-mansion. I'm seeking a lost friend, the broken slate giver of my youth, through directories' meshwork of references, trying to connect her surname; but am informed her address no longer exists. Another farm uprooted by urban sprawl, I'm dreaming. She could have lived in suburbs — until a radical change like a new road, a new style. That old library was built to last to be a disperser of books forever, like the names cut in glass over a door to a doctor's surgery that defies mortality, against the fickleness of kings and queens. Fatigued by officialdom, frustrated with lists, I return to the coffee bar. Notice its number is the same as the address she long ago gave me, a coincidence of sorts that might have perplexed Swedenborg. I make excuses for fate, soliloquising that numerals may, past understanding, correspond to the relationship between two people or ideas. Such calculations often elude the heart too, or leaves us bewildered with the potential of our dreams. We know it's a trick of light on marble inscriptions, a tease to bring us back for a second day, to have routine probability mock us again. Ah, I'm too eager to leave, consign all to the impossible. Where do these scribbled exposed reflections come from: why her, why then, that distant place, this heart-ache?

Just before rush-hour waiting for a bus

a girl's cheek-glow
shies from a window
washed by trickles

It's not her, she's in her late twenties, thirties, but the illusion's comforting, enticing as if she might care to be re-discovered if I could find... without having a reason to relocate. Ultimately we let go, something has taught us this.

Homeward, home-bound
after work, on the Aberdeen bus

bronze glints in hand
some passenger's house key drawn
long before 'next stop'

October 15th

At bible study in the house of Ruth's friend.

Nancy's front room looks too comfortable with various shades of
pink.

crocheted blanket,
between cosy armchairs
a tiny life's curled

and we, five, leaf
across tremulous foliage —
faith's unending book

while in dancing white
a china statuette stands near
pink chrysanthemums

Teaching in a Baptist Seminary, Michael and Alison named their first child Tracy.

she breaks opinions,
cradling sobs her dad strolls
rocking with each step

A mystical evening in the midst of materialism yet it seems that religion has become material, and the spirit — like the wind — has fled beyond creed, church and lessons. To where? Not to this pat house, yet who can doubt the owners' sincerity and wish to know and love that spirit. But I sense that these sincere people rarely stand in awe at the vast 'un-script-able' cosmos. Naturally they're interested in being saved — as if the Bible was a work manual for that purpose.

October 16th

Last evening out with Don and Vanessa,
later, on a faithful park bench
faithful to boyhood adventures
but not for misfiring lovers

across midnight
moon-touched, hill-trees roll
to three designs of eyes

The Res

The planked, concrete-cast bench we share is on The Res, nickname for a City Reservoir. Its fathoms unheard, under a green plateau. It squeezes against the pine-roofed Escarpment creating a three-tier ascent. A stone flight of cathedral-style steps leads to a grassed first level that expands to the size of three football fields. Snuggled in corners, under trees, by the enwrapping fence, are cast seats viewing points towards my childhood and onwards. On the small second level, bronze clumps of shrubs and a horizontal path divides the upper from the long lower slope. A frightful toboggan run in winter, the path becomes a launch pad for a leap into space. Usually back then we pre-teen-dare-devils chose the east end's long slope, a graded track that gave a humbler plunge. Though on that tilt, my younger brother broke his leg. I and fellow tobogganners carried him home on our shoulders, a wounded warrior, laid out; with his leg kept aligned. At home, blamed for disobeying my dad's 'don't you go sledging' I was also praised for bringing my brother home, on the toboggan, his injured limb kept straight. At the Res's west exit, from a black tunnel, water gushes. On my solo exploits, I peered into that slimy, dark smelling hole, longing to find from where the stream came, wanting to trace it back. Beyond that out-flow, past the meadowy tall grass and milkweed fringes, the steep wilderness began leading on to the rapids at Chedoke Creek, the Grand Canyon of my juvenilia. The Res was less stern, but reaching its third domain — that upper platform — looked difficult and dangerous: what lurked there? Too close to whitish cliffs, beyond my sightline? At last a solid teenager, I played football on that high field, lunging for a mis-aimed pass. Nose-diving into a bed of pink peonies, I marvelled at their beauty, was slow to return to the game. Later, elite companions talked, shared heady philosophies, under the blossoming Crabapple, Golden Chain, Toba Hawthorn and Maple. In summer heat by mitten-leaved margins, we lounged on the mown surface and discussed. It was to here, I replied, when my first passion asked 'where shall we go?' on our one night of freedom. Across the Res as if all I knew of love-making was to reveal this haunt of my innocence — when along the salamander way, on bare-knee jaunts, I would lever rocks to catch one, wondering if its tail would come off in my hand, or not.

October 17th

Final evening, penultimate day

From different sources, from wide-ranging homes and promises, my family visits. We enjoy an easy-time party: my brother Don and his wife, Jackie, who plays the violin and viola and their daughter Elizabeth; Cousin Judy with George, parents of my godson, Scott. George, that good man, who never says an ill word to me and Judy my first life-saving cousin-friend. We, all of us, sit and nibble, drink and talk, reminisce while making future arrangements circled by the vivid onus and phenomenon of the present. Its demands. A harvest, the abundant room crowds in around us (only stationary a moment like the glass-makers work, a kind of shining artificial orchard) loaded with grandfather's things. Antiques he brought from England or his keen eyes purchased here. Furniture, he, a cabinet maker for sixty years, created for mum and our family or for his own spacious home which his wife loved, inspired and endured: a statue — Diana the huntress, two wooden stools, Don's and my names inscribed. They repose, under one roof, all the objects my mother as an only child has inherited, before, at her death, they'll be dispersed to who knows where? In response, my father has gained a passion for collecting antique clocks bringing a new one home from each of their journeys to Europe and further across the globe...my dad and mum the most unexpected globe trekkers. We're in limbo a few hours, stranded, indoors, dream-storms outside, waiting — our voyages behind us or stretching ahead — we're held in the happiness allowed, among the miraculously recovered, the yet unborn, the long departed, the familiar and already strange, the selfish and selfless acts that accumulate over decades until they become items we could handle, polish and move around for best vantage, off the mantel on to the sideboard then a chess-board-designed table with a tickle-me-open drawer which outwitted my many child-attempts.

the big room wisps...
joining-in tall cases tick-tock
across our word-ings

October 18th

Photograph of my grandparents
'Papa' and 'Grandma'

old companions
from a shared frame look
beyond octaves

domiciled a month
yet summer to summer
some leaves unturned

For Elizabeth

your finger-print smear
on mum's polished glasswork (thanks!)
assists my 'so long'.

On the Return Flight to England

Remembered from the cottage
hoping to see the Aurora Borealis prance
across the sky...

beaver's tail slaps —
below voluptuous stars
the leanest wake

Last night
when all had gone home, and dad to bed,
the post-party washing-up done, the house
regaining its mercurial silence and peace,
as if she'd taken on my role my mum
was clothed in the trappings of the outsider
who keeps weird hours, who burns the candle
at both ends, singeing his fingertips like a chain
smoker, a writer, a witness who must always listen
whose court appearance is endlessly deferred
my mum against all her conventionality, stirred
perhaps by love or fear of loss, or acceptance
hugs a chair and wants to hear my thoughts

she's the rarest guest
our talk deepening
through small hours

Returning from North Bay
re-entering the sphere of past experiences
I recalled a forgotten girlfriend
and all the misunderstandings
I couldn't explain away or heal...
maybe excessive coins in a phone box were
less important than another's heart
everything suddenly jangles
in a luxury upholstered car...

why didn't she trust me to be
where I said I would be?

dad's Olds ninety-eight
zooms along holiday streets
wild with teenage grief

Taxiing, ready to leave Canada

festooned with jewels
the lady beside me calls
'bye bye nice city'

The phrase echoes my mother's fateful words, driving away from the cottage near Buckhorn, filled with a longing to return and return 'goodbye little house'.

Space-voyagers

twin engines gleam:
as if steadying us
a circular moon

From Toronto 'Departures'

my dad and mum
like pillars prop each other,
brief space between

Ruth

I hug my sister
her swirly hair buried
in disappearing arms

I have learned I teased Ruth for wearing glasses when a girl and I
a six years older brother. Now under-breath I praise her fragrance
wishing I could be on two sides of the Atlantic. Each return reveals.
I'll have to live years as if I had never left my homeland. Everything
that has happened in absence or ignorance needs to be addressed
and redressed if possible. The road not taken will require custom
duties from the other pathway that appeared chosen.

On the oceanic flight back to the UK I think: my stay — an
intimate-alien's, who must know and not know origins and survive
the paradox. My September arrival, its first-leg past industrial
acres and green belt, past shrubby throw-off sites and traditional
homesteads, forecast complexities I would meet each day and night. I
faced my home's many-sided windows, encountered its intersections
with stop lights or not, or with red octagon all-ways stops. My city's
variations no more controlled than oscillations in woods, by lakes
or among warbling birds. As the month motored by, perspectives
opened and closed in beguiling ways, leaving my heart floundering
and delighted. My travel sketch closes with so little resolved. Who
needs a finale, a disclosure, when the Europe-bound jet will skid on
to new worlds? When my feet touchdown at Manchester Airport
already I have promised to return.

Father, Mother and Canada

Leaving Canada

The thirties' high-speed locomotive, in stone
relief, headlines the C.N.R. station, now trackless,
where the city slopes towards its long-discoloured bay
where, rucksack and a case underarm, I left my home —
mum and my puffy-eyed grandma seeing me off.
We must've taken a twilight cab as none of us drove,
neither of them anticipating I might never return.

In semidarkness, we waited on the hardest bench
my escorts' hands folded in mine soft as a pudding
with their spring-scented wrists and lipstick smiles.
The Atlantic-bound was late. After months and years
of planning, for a moment, it seemed I might not leave.
Then a gust of air whistled; couplings flexed into place:
from the pull-down window waved a wave I can't retract.

Stranger Returns Home

for John Sutherland

'Whose hands I can no longer clasp'

Mum, please never expect me
to understand how long your
heart sorrows might linger for his
for your star-aligned love. Only

only at clear dawn among his room's
shiny hoard of unwound clocks,
I recall my dad's, your husband's
labour to keep them tick-tocking.
Each day he inserted precision
keys and finessed filigree hands.
Now, gilt cornered with bugling
cheeked seraphim, as four winds
from Georgian or Regent Eras, now
his each clock face looks mis-timed.

At noon, the passenger door's
pulled to with a retiring thump
and our journey begins. I grip
the white steering wheel as
he might've and indicating
slip out into the spring traffic.
En route, at your street's far end,
we pass a rambling shambolic house
tall with its unresolved roof angles
with discordant doors and windows
I've known since being a child:
out front its magnolia in bloom.

About five miles away at his grave
ground's stone mouth we curve by

the cemetery's one bleached statue
a robed saviour with arms up-lifted
like a huge-winged bird descending.
A little later, once struggling from
the passenger seat into partial light,
at last you let your fragile hand settle
a ninety year old leaf on my shoulder:
a touch, I wish could never be blown away.

Beside his small bronzy inscription
I'm scared to think: it appears he just
passed through this 'neck of the woods'
(to use his locating phrase) had no time
to plant a lasting impression, a home.
But you point out his resident signing
'That life service emblem's his'
sunlight detailing the shared plaque,
'and this one's mine', you put in,
remembering sixty years ago
how you threw in your lot
with this de-mobbed man ...
and now into the afterlife.
I remember how someone
pinned a royal legion brooch
to his suit's lapel when he rested
in his open coffin four years back
unable to resist or salute.

'Here', you direct, 'we set down
a wreath last winter.' I muse on
underneath that massing snow
how far down that circle could've
reposed, washed out, disarranged
how deep too he must have slept,
below that packed white as if piled
overhead sprawled one more earth

to have to shout through. But now
more easily disturbing, perhaps,

in green May, his dying time,
we can hear him speak to us —
his aphasic family with one language.
His corny jokes missed and tongue
tied all his teams sportsman rooting.
I stoop, dragging from trouser pocket
my wasted whitish handkerchief
dampening a corner with my tongue
attempt to wipe away, along his
and your metal lettering, the already
ground-in, discolouring dust and grit.
He comprehended better than any
of us that gravity towards the fallen.
He shared something with his comrades
that even you admitted you didn't know.
I shone his metals on his funeral day.
You chose his unwed, young recruit's
portrait for the town paper's obituary.

The big highway almost blocks out
a high-perched red-wing blackbird
enquiring: 'who was he? 'who was he?
who who who who was he?' as if
from a marching jingle. Against
the military image, I recall his artistry
from boyhood, teenage memories
that commitment he had to make
something, anything from materials
as varied as driftwood, glass and copper.
His trade wasn't clock nursing,
or kiboe or rifle duty cleaning.
He threaded alloys, linking pipes
to make a home's water-veins plumb;

rubbed soldered elbows until un-jagged
and connections firm, nothing left to chance
('there's no such thing as an accident', his refrain)
then gazed on — what he named his monuments.

After his working man years
(fallen into wealth by lottery)
retired, he joined the Order of St John
then reckoned they were another brand
of upper class bigots, and left their red
and white flags, gripped his fatherless roots

again. He could drop a job, down tools,
for justice's sake, come home to flower-aproned you
with a vacant pay packet, (four kids to feed)
and believe he'd nurture us
beyond any boss' jim-trickery,
coupled with that almost comic warning
in his scansion: 'don't act
like you've been
hatched in the sun
on a fence post.'

Skilled maintainer, master, rebel, soldier...
as if to know should resolve grief.
'I like valleys [a pause] more than mountains'
he once declared disrupting mine
and a tour guide's aspirations. He staked
his homeland as 'God's own Country'
the best territory and as the years
passed got more and more tetchy
about leaving to visit any-where-else —
wanting his last sighting to be home.

His wish was granted. Today,
no grey and white Canada geese
groom or repose among interment

plaques that first set level with the here
and now; appear over years to begin
to sink and tilt changing the terrain
as if distorting time. This long hour
with so little to distract, you

love bent, stick bent over,
more than I could ever imagine,
mum, a thin secluded figure
you start retreating, slip unaided back to his
Chevrolet Impala's comfy-seat shelter,
(part of his legacy) with a cushioned clunk
pull the door behind you, as if locking
out the facts, the whole damn show.
You leave me to enquire from me:

how long can I stand looking
down at this trap-door to the dead?
Do I wish it would open?

The normal rites and grieving
hours have passed and his honour
and whatever his dues, lapsed and
insurance policies have matured. His
stocks no longer require watching.
But his, that metamorphosis, stays
fresh and candid as when first
buried as if he is incorruptible. His
ending transforms aging and time,
(no more dying or clock-watching)
giving the scented hope, the prospect
that death, anyone's final departing,
is at last the perfected response
to life that few if any can rehearse.
And I suspect no mourner, staring
at their nervous feet, feels at peace
with the stagey earth as a destination

wind-howled to rock or dust-muffled
it remains a stranger to every soul.

'What's the purpose of dust?' a flushed
conservator once asked, as if her trained
assurance had snapped shut like a coffin.
I shied from saying it hides our undoing,

each one's 'shattered nerves' and wreckage.
It's good that we can take nothing with us.
Feel — even what we leave behind is veiled.

Off a ways, a small party
on the humpy horizon hazily huddle
at a newly arranged burial; they've
chosen an upper knoll plot, black their
dominate colour. I share, allowing
my mind to wander, to attenuate
out across to be with that family,
friends and once a life companions
who show up on this day and
are never seen again. Together,
as if a spontaneous community,
they stand mute in a roughened ring
and see, by unstinting shovel-thumps,
how the entire brown earth appears
to close-in round their casket and

simple love…'Come back to the living!'
dad's dated alarm echoes in my ears;
he'd shake the earth if he could.
On command, I turn toward
the car. Mum, you, missing his
raised voice, stare at me perplexed
why I'd taken so long to return.

Mum in Her Nineties

coming to be ageless

I

In your easy chair, up close
your face — as if a cat clawed
your skin but too gentle
for blood to ooze.

What's coming of age
when no longer dying your hair
denying the years
and reliance on beauty
are past
and you can claim
nothing's wrong
except growing old?

You might complain
first I was beautiful
then motherly
next a prop for my husband
then alone.

You've left
the leafy mainland
I'll tell you that
you're a peninsula's tip
soon to be broken off
a white wraith island
I won't be able to tell you that.

Now we share the back room settee,
by the big window towards the garden

that acts a door in warm weather;
the season mostly scraped

we share the shoe-lace tied albums
as more leaves cascade outside
photo after photo plate
turning the black felt leaves;
you want me to accept —
not to interrupt
with that's strange, that's
too intriguing, who's lusting who
there — ? you want me to bow
to your history, the highlights
— whether the image is
over-exposed, framed
by a rippled white space
in black and white or colour
a rectangle or almost square
if a tree grows from
someone's head, if feet are missing
or there's a frown
on the protagonist
on the subject and no one says 'cheese'
too bright, too dim
they're stone markers
to the past
whatever past —
pointing the way
that you took, have taken
and you want me to embrace them
as if how you became you
is how I became me.

What I want to know
is: where does the glamour
the movie star gestures —
angled bare legs to the thighs —

on the back steps — go?
Where does quick-march
off the mark in a business coat
rushing to work on time
where does your Mondays downtown
end up — escaping us kids, paying bills
preparing the tasks ahead
perhaps sneaking a treat;
your arithmetic skills,
doing the taxes, managing the budget,
and you hated cooking
but you cooked some fine dishes
on Fridays,
where does your duties go
when none can be repeated,
is left to history
and are cherished in each picture
in each pictorial prompt
as memory...?

You remember less and less.

Mum, you've out-survived
your friends; who'll grieve
who'll plant your wreath
like an ancient bridal bouquet
tossed without hope
who'll kneel to polish your half
of the iron-red name burial plaque?

II

We're still in the back room
on the settee together
and you repeat
'there's nothing wrong with me'.

No pain or distress in your silver-grey wave
that shimmers twice monthly-fashioned
above a more and more cratered

subdued face
cheeks collapsed that
yet puff out a command
for me to lift my head
and not sink
in my bewilderment
at this or that imperfection.

You ask under breath
'why did he have to leave'
meaning me

and say... 'the burning bush
you should've seen it
yesterday'

but add
'there wasn't enough rain'
'this summer to bring out
the reds before winter'.

Your fine-shaped garden
lies under plummeted leaves
brunette peaked and crinkling up
up to statued Diana's ankle

with its huntress fragrance
lingering that swoosh your stick-aided
feet made by a tumbled wall
where once desirably
smooth-skinned,
you'd desired to lay

down without your tiara
and accept fate.

To live with nothing wrong
how can that be called fate?

All you know for sure — is
a voice that came from upstairs
from the peaked ceiling room,
after the hard-time parties,
the violence and the soldiers
crept home and tried to pretend
they'd never left.
'Come up,' the voice said.
'We need a foursome' it confirmed.
You saw the future love of your life
sat behind kings, queens and jacks.

Through the back window
from your easy chair, yellows
and oranges look perfect
before descending.

Yours' a perfecting (I guess)
that looks like it can't hold on
another second, yet re-awakes
each first light still from a double bed
and reads and reads far into the night
clinging day after day.

There seems a refining
in your dying (dare I call it that)
in rouge painted nails
that can no longer marshal needles
to knit a Fair Isle yoke sweater
or make smocking for a daughter's dress,
in your too velvety right hand

that can't grasp a pen to write
a letter to an outcast

and you remember less and less
who seems to have outlasted life
edging to immortality's brink.

Fragments of your maytime
are chased across the blacktop
drive, unable to repose on this
or the other side, but you want
to garner them like radiant snapshots
or a pack of cards
shuffle out their truth.

In your poised waiting
since you almost do nothing you say,
except the ironing on Tuesdays
and loading the dishwasher sometimes
you mystify your attendant me
though you tell him everyday facts
and assure him the history
has been documented
in photographic love
still he asks aside —
how will you cast
your widow's will?

Your off-spring argue
over a famed in-laid table
you say nothing.

On the home walls
are fastened certificates
in burnished frames
to your life-long service
to this and that

and somewhere pinned
your unending service
to me, your first son...

When I break the polite code
and mention the exit clause...

'I'm 93, it can't be long.'

'What do you think
is beyond life, mum?'

'I don't know'
in a voice more sunk-cheeked
than a whisper
'I try not to think about it'.

You prefer
each existence's nervous
piece in a tree's cleft
or on a roof's tile
to that solid unknown beyond.

Yet you manage an alchemy.
Your wrinkle-encircled eyes
no longer observe leaves
falling but autumn petals
not grounded or venerable
but blooming in space
from a flower's invisible greens.
Look! A black squirrel leaps
from one creased bare branch
to another on your tall maple
as you speak of nearby trees
as your final friends.

And your face looks cracked
lined as that century-old maple's bark
but unimaginably soft.

III

Later, I watch you descend
from the second floor
ease yourself downstairs,
rugged step after step — backwards
you grip the tanned handrail
the other hand presses into wallpapered wall —
with your spine's humped curve —
making peace with all descents.

I'm ashamed that I can't reach up
to the sky for you
and shake down its truth.

But who at last will
your frail leaves favour,
where at last settle
on an escarpment's viewing bench,
above a river, on top of a loved one's grave
or in a squirrel's rough-sketched nest?

It's simple your loving
and each photo records
and with 'don't read too much
into anything', you come back at me.
Again we're in the back room
with the tv, cherished books
your souvenirs, heirlooms
and the on shelf albums.
The morning's past away

with its mid coffee break
and her order has settled
relayed from pink creased lips
and a jewel dotted neck
but now she's silent and
can't help but marvel
why her son-petitioner looks longingly
at the neighbourhood roof-scapes
and loves to hear her wind chimes ring.

Snow Around The Lake of Bays

Lifting toward the Haliburton Hills, too serene
bare arching limbs weigh densely lined in white.
Tall spruce, pine and cedar carry the fallen mass
wear epaulettes without a sign of war or triumph.
Bendy roads, ploughed a ways, lead to dark ruts
along clover leaf bays, between smoothed banks
to window-bright-cottages decorated for a brief age.
Between converging slopes, into an unseen cleft
the day-light fades, looks to descend. Streamers —
in paling purples, cerised-reds and quiet ambers —
waver from in-shore waters out to the lake's heart
as if all the known landscape is being pulled back
lured far out of reach, until nothing can rescue it.

Nipissing Twilight

Lake Nipissing's cold and dark surges moan
against stacked rocks, in gaps, with deep gulps.
Its angled whitecaps rise; their whipped spray
glazing with ice the dock's shored up boulders.
On horizon, a blaze hints in orange-ochre cloud.
Each wave coats the ticket cabin in a glassy sheet.
From far away glints, a northern night advances.
And through the extended portrait of banded isles
over hill-lines, scraped and scoured by glaciers,
its retinue edges near, blanking the southern sky.
Old snow has thawed, but the air predicts frost
as in turquoise mauves the speckled light dims.
A first star's set to pierce the dying wind's peace...
moored, up the beach, sight-seeing boats at peace.

The Heirloom

Today, as if from reverie, my aged mum
revealed a first edition of *Alice's Adventures
in Wonderland*, that she had used through
her only-child childhood as a colouring book —
its first plates liberated from the binding,
its cloth cover torn to its rudimentary heart
in places, and its maroon surface blistered.
In yellows, blacks and browns or red dashes
she'd crayoned over fine-pen border designs
portraying Charles Pearl's Edwardian Alice
in purple, by the Fish Footman, a blue swiggle.

A 1910 edition, bought, when she'd reached
four or five or six, second-hand, by her father
now squeezes in between unscarred hard backs.
Amazed, she excites that the book's survived
through decades and recurrent chucking outs:
auctions and flea markets, including her own,
had outlasted her desire for revenge against
her long deceased dad for the valued objects
he gave her; then affectionately teased back
realising he'd earn a good price for the thing,
money for her needs along with lapsed promises.

Poor Alice bears her defacing, mis-colouring,
without reproach, but with an absurd knowing —
the naivety that mum's dad loved and hoped
his one child, into womanhood, would pursue
adopt unreason and awe against logic's court
the way he gazed yearningly at a tree's shimmer
for no cause, an artist gaze that craved nothing.
Or what did he desire against his impermanence?
Time-marred, colour scored pages: his daughter
beyond some dealers' estimating, scribbled her
annotations for the next keen reader to decipher.

Six Dinner Guests

Through a May afternoon's
dull splattering
         we meandered to a feast
seat-belted in a cream SUV
a table secured
at nicknamed Average Joe's.

Through plate glass, Trout Lake
lapped.
Fish or flesh, we gave his or hers
separate order
         drink cubes chinked
in a ruby Caesar
         Niagara wines, ginger
ale, apple cider and a coke
         we chattered on.
One rainbow's sinking beam
         shifted
over a birch tree's mask
tailed off toward streaks
         titivating
some of the continent's
         oldest hills.
The youngest guest relayed a story
from a friend's pal who had seen...
and we puzzled for a second
if six hundred feet down in the lake's
crevice if something vast, sleek
         pulsated
         past glacial debris.

The cuisine superb
         almost every plate clean
we rose, gathered to leave

our reflections mobbed
                    window views.

The owner with bizarre finesse
                        held up
our coats
        by the shoulders
        like pelts
        and placed them on us
one by one.

Outside, along the spruce and
                  white pine inlets
we half-heard creatures forage
                    feeling
we could never share in their night
        secrecies
but knew   somehow
        we fed on them and they on us

just a scattering now
        who splashed from spurs
or finned their way into coves.

We trailed
alongside gravel parking slots
each hooded engine lulled,
lidless head lamps
surveyed the marina.

Then up the timber dock
a girl thundered   in a two-piece
      both hands lifted
with a huff   flung a huge stone in
scampering back
           her white top rippled.

Down, submerged, below disturbance,
  in fissures   a slick beast
dragon and fish combined
                    a monster slid
and darted to devour
                consumed imagination.

Nipissing Stillness

The afternoon pontoon ship plies. Engines purr. A giant feline carries me to the sunny islands. Water moves in patterns of stillness, like long radio waves, in flights of slight corrugations. Each low swell a far expanded wing. Sand flies envelop the Chief Commanda II, named after the chiefs of the Nipissing people going back to the War of 1812. The insect swarm doesn't bite. Other boats alter the delicate fluid designs, timid uniform swells parallel at times across the open blue-greyness. Creases, shaving nicks, mark the lake's face. Water-skin crinkles, no white caps or peaks or troughs. The ferry pushes on, through heat, crossing formations, cross-paths of invisible birds. Quietude deepens. The high sun builds tall water-pillars that shimmer and vanish into the depths. A shallow lake easily aroused, so placid. Nearing the five islands its appearance changes, dim movement annotates the tranquillity. One landfall slides past, off the port, revealing further drops of green earth in the background. Serene varied greens, white sandy beaches. A flotilla of ducks pass between the islands in the distance a black line moving across the haze. The biggest island un-touched, a broad-leaved forest down to its shore, a floating plateau of the Precambrian shield. In the straits the surface adornment changes to minute ribs of plaid. Sacred islands carry in turn a curse. Story of starvation after war, a native woman with special powers sent to bring help and returns to the islands to see all its dying survivors gone, not a trace, not of bodies, of belongings or of violence. A caldera of volcanoes millenniums ago gives the shaped quintet an insular symmetry. No wave-white breaks around rocky out-posts. 'Islands of the Sky' look blood-bound by a hidden desire. Unbeached lands. Sound of silence is playing in the lost background from the cruising boat's horned loud speakers. Taunt lines, wrinkles, aging marks, sound marks: the half-waves resemble moving backs of abundant shiny fish. Lines cross-hatch; the lake's pointed with wispy chain mail, each subdued rise and fall joined. Minor ripples over the deeper oscillations, each flowing miniature blemish like a scratch. The engine kneads, and claws, the boat turns from The Mantious back towards its home harbour's speech. Unhindered light creates the mirage of glowing curtains, like a reversed Northern Lights, rising from rolling passivity. Cirrus reflected in a unified stream; the wake's intricate white beading trims the constant dark-blue-grey. Suddenly tranquil water of Nipissing is intimate with my dreams.

from 'Red Hawthorn-Hedged'

IV

When did I first long for the here and now?
I stared for miles from the rear side window
of my father's car; saw the moon
for the first time as free
a winged horse in silver disguise,
motoring as fast as dad's Pontiac
far advanced in age. Comfortable
in that tasselled-textured backseat
I had no yearning to return home.
I filled up with all that I watched
the rear glass' soft curve sharing
curved muscles of that night-galloper.
I begged the journey not to end.
Here I am, after decades of journeys
gazing from a train's round-cornered glass
still hoping for non-arrival, the sacred
in-between-ness of here and now.

From the Passing Window

He saw forests, deep forests, nameless lakes, but the forests weren't deep. Facades for the tourist/traveller; logging companies had scooped out the interior and left a skin of tall trees. The lakes had lost their teeming fish that the others, those First Nations had speared and netted — their waters once honoured and named. He didn't have a name for those inhabitants, or used the wrong word full of misrepresentation. Then a traveller through northern forests, he thought of her, not those who had lived for many centuries in the terrain. How long would we last and call those ice-thin lakes nameless? He wasn't interested in the big we but the small intimate we. It was late October. She was in the city he'd left. He was in Tom Thompson country; the season the mood the same for hundreds of years. Snow didn't hang from branches but radiance clung in reds, purples, gold, yellows, silver, oranges, blacks and green — love colours (he thought) when far from his love. He was out away across an unbroken territory, past Great Lakes, across their northern edge towards Prairies. Two days later half asleep in the observation car mountains reared by like Cyclops; they crowded the sky, in love, pressing upward to a resolution. Nothing would be the same again. He didn't know that. At dawn, down a gorge tallest firs appeared. First on the other side of the mountains, then the sun filled the river long before a drop was felt through his passing window.

He heard her last words fade. Her green short skirt's light swish. Did he hear a tear — which he left unrescued? The trees made little sound; too cold to open the glass. He must've listened through blankness. Inside, underneath, the huge metal snake with its hiss passed through outer silence. He heard the artist's brush strokes on canvas, the canoe's paddle, the lover's kisses, brush smack, amorous smack. The wheels underside, lower down on the steel rails the snake rushed, clicking and clacking; heard the rail miles lengthening. She'd spoken and ripped through his virgin land that wished for and rejected the human. Back in the city her settee had spoken her skirt, not her — she let him go. His feet were suddenly on the pavement outside her house. Proudly he left, yearning adventure. It was night on the street, an owl. Then the steel wheels reminded there was no turning back to her room of silence. 'Why didn't you say stop, I don't want you to leave.' Didn't her tears mean that? What else could they have meant unexpected on her blushed face? Antics of passengers worked their distraction and he, in an upright seat, squeaked, squirmed for a relaxing position to sleep to forget, no curtained berth. He was forced to listen to aligned stars speak in night's fearful muteness and speak more loudly.

He pressed so close to the window he believed he smelt the passing forests, grain fields, cliffs and water that white plunged or rested black yet glittered surrounded by its dark audience. He smelt seat leather and a creeping winter sweat of his unchanged clothes and scanty washes. The cabin hot, the train a barrier against the unknown. Tasted the steam's hiss and breathed in faint but there was a lover's dividing kiss, fragrance of someone's flowers down aisle, and food being served, when he had money for five meals in five thousand miles. Surely he devoured the scent of oil, oil's insistence to grease the passage, keep shiny points speeding past; carriages/cars joined, so they didn't clash but race over the rails towards other smells: an ocean's oily waves in a harbour city and broken glass and the night smells of the pained city. He wasn't there yet. Was still almost sane, not yet arrived. En route and full of romance enclosed in love's scent of fear and distrust. Why didn't he trust her, but left her best fragrance. She gave up much. He recalled that night they walked around the reservoir as if walked on water, hug after hug; inside her coat her body's perfume sneaking out. It rained against the window, created imaginary smells of distance from her. Can distance smell like they say fear can? What moved Tom Thompson, what scent of non-wilderness? The painter knew it wasn't death but rebirth. The traveller longed for rebirth in the harbour city when his life was behind him in her city on a smelly hump-backed street — her door ready to swing open to his entry.

Against the passing window he felt alone. Out of it. Without her nearness, promise and struggle, her death of his post-teenage youth. Helpless, felt driven, carried. Did he want to leap out at the next minor stop and start to hike back thousands of miles which would've been his death; to carry his coffin his one case, between boulders, through walls? He was without a companion, he'd broken something, crushed by opinion, savaged from within, but excited by ... the journey deceived, towards a destination and no return, the first of his no-returning ways, no home lap or sweet reunion. But after two months in the port city he returned to her street. Came back on a celebratory night. Her door unlocked, he slipped into her house and almost before she could say hello with surprise he slipped his night cold hands down the front V of her sylph dress and touched those hot treasure sacks, fingering right down to her cushy belly button and below. She thought 'have you at last become bold when it's far too late.' He experienced only mountains. No history, nature's candour urged him towards obscurity and disappearance. Yet, couldn't believe he'd chosen separation; ran from love. 'If you had stayed, why didn't you stay and trust me?' Her controlled phrases came, after recrimination and disgust, before a final closing the door. He was an immature journeyer, always not sensitive, not patient, not smart.

In the harbour city he cheated and stole half an hour on the phone for a transnational call to her and blubbered, 'you should be here, should come quick to snatch our black swans from those nameless lakes — our longed for children that we've promised each other'. And she may have come if he'd been patient as the shore rock citadel. It was his destiny to be childless. She then fertile, desperate for good birthing after the flesh had swollen in her body to become a dead thing, dis-formed, stinking, and much cruel secrecy against her. She didn't know the fate of her conception. The doctor, for her own good, said nothing and let her long and long. She told her beloved she wanted everything to change through him. He pleaded, why didn't you cuddle in beside, thigh on thigh, taking in the monster summits beside me? Who knows was her silent reply. He smashed the telephone box to emergency-only-bits with the black receiver's head. Broken, glass-slivers. The windows passing like shimmering scales, the steel reptile; if he could've stood outside and looked as it chug through wedged apart canyons that a century before surveyors and dreamers had discovered, depending on the trail of the indigenous, the first nations, a passage through mountain heights into the hope of creating a new nation. He failed to create love that could last; never seen again, only after many years can be re-echoed against a window side's cataract roar.

On his remembered journey, as if time could be peeled back and the wound re-entered, he asks 'why aren't you sinking into the leather seat beside me, dying a little with each clicketty-click mile, past each landslide and forest-rape?' If only she had abducted him or him her. They were polite like the doctor who wouldn't tell her that her child-to-be would be still-born to keep her from immediate grief and let her experience the horror later. They must be sharing this gazebo of five thousand miles as co-travellers into the unknown through continental nights and days — she a few years, a few centuries older than him; the train aiming with three engines straining between pikes, shrinking to find the passage through, alongside a river, by sheet-lightning cliffs. Their hurrying windows reflected in granite sentinels, in black tree backdrops, in hopeless sky. Be beside me, he says over those tracks, catch small-town commuters and transnational escapees zooming toward new birth, pure form, belief in life. Feel the passion of the contours groaning and rushing. The great coaches with their pyrotechnics taking a deep bend, be excited in love in madness. They, two worms through tireless rock-scape, past breathless views, with a tourist voice, a sight-seer's, ready to leave everything to accompany each other. Don't blame. Come. Buy your ticket. Get on board. Go back forty years plus. Earn your passage, if you can't afford a ticket. Forget home, be a traveller towards death of everything you know for something other.

The creature slinked out of peaks and scars into a vast valley and he felt at the very front, leaning out the window, taking in the vista, as if the driver. The river his companion, the train swerved with its meanders, it led to the ship spotted harbour, the mountains slid like laughing children into the ocean. He had arrived. The big nation finally ended. Would she have been willing to share a five cent bowl of rice begged from the back door flap of a Chinese Restaurant, could she have lived in a bed-sit where out the window the river mist swallowed sense and the urbane and the black swans took flight? Re-follow the locomotive's progress back towards our love. He thinks. Wake up early, shift your beautiful body off the settee, see your shadow ripple on the ocean. How could he know that journey moving like liquid from there to there would cast the die of his life, how that brief failed passion would narrow prospects, infiltrate his dreams? Some things don't expire; their impact gestates, sets a theme. They take new shape but reinforce the design. Has she, since then, like him, been childless? Come to the shatter-proof glass; like the poet says — look if you can, a moment, look out from the passing window at the deep forest of ourselves.

Far From the City

I idle in the small, snowdrift-circled home
of my best friend I have known fifty years.
Through open drapes' cold globe morning,
sun rays dazzle his unlit, ceremonial Pine.
From scented limbs charmed objects hang,
blue, purple, red, memory's random planets.
Still a child's paper chain, toy rocking horse
& hand-carved snowflakes keep their secrets.
Across the room, his 'glass things' that in his
twenties he blew & shaped from molten matter,
still rest on wall-shelves. Tallest swirled vases
& many coloured bowls — his daring creations —
appear to wait their time in the speckled silence.

Seven Earth Odes

I

By The Grave Of Naheebahweequay

Can this long uncared-for site be an image
for a voice that continues without echo …?

After, with soil-claggy fingers, we'd thumbed-in
hollyhocks, and nocturnal earth was compacted,
beyond the first killing frost they still exist
green, wavering by a Princess' grave.

How could she forget the earth,
once the sacred blending of soil had been performed
and inhumed inside this tableau of wonder
as matted bits of frost glistened on the disturbed ground?
Yet, once that persona, human, was no longer embodied,
what known element could detain her disappearance?

Or how can this be signed as her territory
that at the glance is vanquished
a boundary-marking
or ceremony infringed
a sacred mountain tunnelled through?
Yet, it's hard to envisage
that at one time this was her domain,
to embrace the customary ease a perpetual kiss
perhaps lighted on her face; to picture
blues which may've wrapped water and sky;
or greens, the unbelievable impassé
the great forest rolled-up.
Stature of trees and their intimate collapse:
how did she mature among these unscaleables?
When day was twilighted,
what instructed her return
night barely missing to entice
(by a wayward caress she could fall asleep forever)?

What small fears chased her home? And her creed,
a chipmunk's, I imagine.

Let's acknowledge the past. All of us,
we possessed it
and cuddled impossibles,
the unseen persons,
or were vast-winged birds.
Quickly it's changed,
our arms yanked from joints,
spoken of as little liars
we're forced to admit
we only imagined.

There were those who vowed they understood
who claimed they could let her return to every presence
she'd intuited: to her immense terrain, to miniature forms
that better than themselves had perceived her,
to moving wings of sound out of extreme night,
to echoing creatures.
They believed they could let her return
to all she'd described as never-diminishing:
to her inviolable faith
to the arcane, out-loosening dark,
though they cut, and raised up from earth
a tablet of stone
to recount that among them
she'd once lived.

I'm late to desire
a site of anamnesis, a sliver of time,
one window ajar or split in the seam,
some half-opened door to trip the blind
and stumble back.

In a church's precinct
between gateway and porch-light, the guests were late.

Not wishing to disturb. Once we tried to hurry off
but apprehensions settled
and we had to intrude.
But don't use the occasion to appear too unaware
if in the real we could've never troubled a moment
that with or without us it went on
the whole... the expectancy
an unvoiced serenity.
For a quick turn full of grimacing smiles
the room welcomed or barred the way
but our speechless
un-thought, that any circumstance might
out-distance our arrival
that despite us, a frantic serenity would advance
and more far-fetched in the banishment of life
some manner of being would unfurl,
indefinitely, from us.

Remember, chide the nervous feet and walk straight in.

Ancestors, believe us: we live for those minor works.
We'd sweat
to plunge down harder
making the scintillating top
twirl faster
to release animals from their inscribed forms
once they all run
vanished in whirling bands of colour...
as though a Saturn...
with rings of bright reds, yellows and golds
spinning on the air
and faster, a sweet zinging against the ears.
It has to crash, or wobbling on axis
over-tilt, out of control, till collapsed
with little to tell its old planetary self.

Do not devalue an old fable,
like a black boy harassed by tigers
till in an instant tautly held circles
were subsumed and tigers running
too fast churned into butter.
Believe, it was enough, after a nightmare
before sleep, uncertainty reposed on the tongue.

Call this abandoning reason
but let's come once to that chosen site
of unkempt grass and rusted railing
where a Princess' faith
her transliteration
is hinted on stone
and once more, this time absurd with flowers.
It was on the day of our second arrival
that deed over-rode us.
Hearts high, flung too far ahead; quick as it was guessed
snapped themselves round
to retrieve us.
We stepped back, dumbfounded
that we had needs. We wrestled with bewildering things.
Everything had changed.
Unspeakable thoughts
wings
whirlwinds of imagination: uncalled-for
came the guidance of a butterfly and alien figures
        moved on stones
and fates, uncountable fates,
overran our observance
and without courtship, hollyhocks
rushed upon us.

Don't contemplate this — as the grieving of the insane
we recognised their gentleness
and were intrigued by each other's virtue
or should it be misclaimed as love

but on that single day, with trowels
we overturned the yet unfrozen ground
and set down flowers.
They resist the autumn change
and face the shifting cloud-line
(stretching too high to be numbered among nature's naïve)
in a gust, swinging over
backwards — to preserve
what's offered as farewell —
they may hold it.

Since such numbers have disappeared
and continue unaccounted-for,
we dare to enquire, 'from here,
where did her departure lead…?'
No reply suffices from any element. Princess,
you deny inquiry, you've no need to respond.
No more disputing. Nor can we disguise before you
the final passion of the old, to be found small and comfortable
among the household totems
to see who does return
of all who promised
they would.

But you, Princess, handing yourself on entirely
held nothing back for a ghost to be formed.

II

Hallowe'en

In anxious connivance with night
we announce ourselves.
Ignited visions
candled pumpkins cut
through window-panes ablaze against the air.
Jack-o-Lanterns are you prepared for this dark?
You appear to have come from inside a nocturnal world
and hard pressed to force a way out
you shatter into a thousand segments.
Such faces turn against us that we ache
to make a face back.
We must gather speed, swimming the evening air
raiding on with stolen treasures.
Let's be picked up as black coat-tails hurled
forward in a gust.
Take us by all means
bumped and bruised by ghosts and goblins
we're ready for this night.

We change on our feelings...

Always affronting the limits
we want to know what can be
endured and what may not.
Numerous streets are committed to blackness
where there's never enough illumination.
Tell us what's wrong.
We, whipping glances one to next
not half afraid as we should, seem initiated —
for this night. Our costumes fit,
no button-twines unravel or sleeves contract,
covered on all sides, with nothing left bare,
demons can pass unnoticed and take possession.

Don't let me believe this ritual must endure forever.
Nor do I want to scream unrestrained.
Can we never be enrolled with day's disappearance
recognise our terrors
and puzzle out this old Jack-o-Lantern?

Not solely for desire's adventures, but for endurance
that we may take command of our sight
and muscles instep, pulsing
toward an incredible terminus;
between streetlights, goading us on, through missed footfalls,
to places undiscovered,
for a time to acknowledge
the body's throbbing impetus
eager to leap from our eyes
and devour our world.

Father, you may've been devoted
but it hardly seems you were present.
Still, I struggle to keep pace and street-meander
with children, their escapades be through me this night
since there persists enormities of sorrow
emotions pulled up and hurled down when nothing
was remembered long before myself had been formed.
Inexplicable conflicts, between you and I.
Father, couldn't something appease us?

Childhood's content when booty directs our will.
With much gold stashed we race outside
with short work required the front door flies open,
only to make a face at it,
to deceive the front steps, sliding down into shadows
we believe ourselves masked for the getaway.
But we never discerned
life would hurricane through us,
how we would age, like scarecrows up-rooted in a night.
All at once arms thrust beyond sleeves

we're thrown through nocturnal space,
crashing headlong into the current
of remarks and gestures passers-by exchange.
All we never disputed begins to dissemble;
costumes, which once disguised
the frail, night swimmer's stroke,
grow tattered till we lose faith.
Voices that sang out
curl up inside and leave us dumb-founded.
How can they suddenly refuse... our names...to utter?
Those props of lies or evasions
(the supporting roles) are knocked away,
it seems nothing favours our performance;
until, distraught with small doubts,
we make a run for it......back to yours.

Often late, in adult night, the old rationale seizes
that after all else — we are solitaires.
Would it finally pacify to conceive you
as once and once only
never to be over-played or pushed off the stage
not to be again....a father?

But diversely related through unknown bonds,
we, as this outlawed night, persevere
if only through the anamorphosis of desire
and still intense from the exertions of nerve
not completely dissolved into the void
like a wind-faded flag or shredded like office paper.
Our favourite pictographs remain to be deciphered.
We: not yet domineered by dictums of history
still permitted a reliance on our own hand's expertise,
naive enough to be on speaking terms with strangers
not yet threatened by thinned walls or troubled by
who is eavesdropping,
tossing about language like a game of catch
as if all were in agreement.

Criticise us, over again, we deserve for times
arrived home late, damage done, lack of respect shown
but never for greed, that already we were lovers
determined to test more streets for their wealth
and the darkness we could outlast.
To sustain a lifetime's sense, the famous extra one,
another hand jerked out from behind the back
as soon as you imagined we'd had enough, when you
dared to expect we were bulging, another hand appeared:
a thousand tricks to keep manoeuvring
never to have to give up our schemes.

If we stagger back, though, by untried passages
to that same imagery, the toffee apple
home and chocolate walled house,
could those who greet us ignore
we've lost the advantage of size,
would neighbours make us ask for what
is rightfully ours,
(a toffee apple, would it be as enticing?)
could people possibly stop short and say no,
would we be asked to leave?

A candle in a pumpkin is extinguished,
the Jack-o-Lantern goes dark.
Crouched in the corner we wonder
was it only greed
that had inspired us toward their threshold again.

Lemurs, fantasies, visions, prevailing
as columns and terrors, standing
inside ourselves: can't we shake them to understand
that also — we exist?

The ritual eclipsed,
another face accounted...we relinquish the night.

III

Sometime For Vincent

He finished his intolerable hours
to bring home more than himself?
But in another incarnation
would roses allow him as much?
Led away from the tabletop's edge
by gradations of colour,
pinks and reds
obscure the sun's abrupt takeover.
Quick as a stuntman's memory
I'm reminded the sun's yellow and the world small:
stretched open, on the desk, a volume of Van Gogh's prints.

They couldn't devolve as far
but for that borderline
cornered, the straightened-cut to his images;
his will of colour confined to harder fitting space.
His stars, like fire-wheels, seem spun.
If the night was ruthless, wind-churned
with storm-cloud, I could understand his vortices,
but the sky's calm.
His cosmos reacts at a chance of friction
firing out its phantoms of light —
each star, a sun dragged through a knot hole
through a pin-hole, they emerge
spiralled in colour, unleashed toward earth,
spun once and set loose on their shunts of passion.

You clear, elite constellations
would have us conclude
you'd nothing to do with it,
that he was the only one irritated
and not you; all his yearning, only

his unconnected nerves spiking
the passive black sky.

See how the city, unconstrained, runs with light,
the straight forward glare
through the untainted glass.
Have one come to our aid and click them all off
gradually light would re-impress
and illuminate our posture
where we leave off and some other begins,
human or margins of a mantelpiece.
Or from an unrealised source
a passage of flames one to the next
might invade the room
or in clear formations as from a diamond-cutter's steady hand
or how children might envisage, five-pointed, elementary
and placed on the top.

It's all done for us... the display of the universe
is already hooked up.

We assume familiarity
to gaze toward your ceaseless pattern
you high motifs of the polished night.

Still, with or without a telescopic lens,
we haven't gathered-in one star-expression. Each glimmer,
from our first sighting, has planted its light far beyond us.

For him it was near incalculable: beyond a stretch of trees
the void thick with strange buoyancy
and stroked and bubbled
each nocturnal glow
streaked up and down.
He could never shake them off
any more than an impaired, speechless girl can, who
with her finger-point on the air, imagines a design.

Her torment, there's no end to her creation.
Her least move only continues its shape;
she can't throw it off, by flicking her hands
or sticking them in her pocket
(her fly-paper touch always more intimate);
it solely increases by lines
the original contorted and made unavoidably hers.

From here, we cherish separation, watching the elements rotate.
From you, far, silent illuminations,
we sight where needled glows dart into black,
then, recognise on lake, puddled surface or
on a pool gleaming momentarily in the palm
of mute hands. Which is your truest mirage —?
The weight of these reflections in constant dispute.
But, at an isolated hour, in open-eyed bloom
roses were assigned the trope of the stars.
Yet, how many others, here, in a certain
earth-moment, have betrayed as much affinity?
The wedding sanctuary filled, seemed
could never be dispersed to darkness.
For two costumed young adults,
(the cause of the room's commotion)
lovers apart, but on each other attending,
a seam of light slipped open to take them in
whilst above the congregated heads
a dance of candles flickered.

You, still more exulted,
by a lingering glance up
are we heightened?
Sometimes, You reduce the infinite in praise of Us,
but let there be no more responses or hushed prayers about it.
On that terminal day, our backs turned,
we'll not be remote enough to renounce
this dressed-up procession down a front aisle
away from the centre, the crepe streamers

sloping from the ceiling, swung lower for doorways;
till we, assembling outside, so abruptly amazed, one of us
might on their tip-toes try to guess the lineage of the stars.

Hey! Mrs. ____. You eked out a recovery.
About your time of discharge
you couldn't shout enough. Then, no one was around
who'd once recorded your taciturnity.
You called yourself by a stranger's name
and gave up on goodnights. You finally recognised
in the all-out gallop of escape from the hospital
you met the always 'worst-off-one'
the young, who floundered, already leaning
on a lifetime of supports.
You're outside her now.
You side with grocery
managers fearing for their arranged shelves
and cashiers or customers
who wait impatiently for her to pass:
she, who, at the first endowment
inside her whirlpool eyes
handled the constant jar of her disordered steps
knocking the finished stars off their pins
(not to be taken for eternal)
who threw the hope never to grow old
back in our teeth.

It can't be saved...a bystander's innocence.
We know better. The frail instruments probe
and goad us on to brute discovery
to the farthest leap of the sky — a million sparkler-ends
turned inside out
as the frisson of colour expands, as the high peaks of fires
burn on the face
and sharpest horizons flare
like blazing firebrands —
night's multitude of suns before the world's demise.

What appears, at a glance, as universal
takes its sightline from a remote intimacy.
But, how could we wait for her return, or endure
the reticence of her black shimmering clothes?
We could only hasten order on to that vanishing form
and break in: are you the once endeared,
among almost forgotten, of first born
that shone through our sleepy windows, tell us,

are you the one?

As tears of alcohol left in an emptied glass
we're filled with afterglow.

After the snuffing out of candles
and the service was concluded
with the flicking on of everyday lights
at the beginning of the choir girls' rehearsal,
after the choir leader had gone over her part
separately and treated mistakes,
pass the act of closing the huge doors and walking home,
after the stairs wound past her parents,
alone in her room, the window raised,
her pearled face
bared against the chilling night
she sang her heart out...Teacher, if you could've
heard her then, unaccompanied,
all the gaps of silence singing
on her tip-toes, her unlevelled voice, the dark warped back...
after this, and the tailing off of her song,
out there...for him it was colour.

IV

The Beloved

Had the trumpeters been alerted
he, in that same night hour, would've come through lost
since she, his beloved,
in a split-second — deserting earth — had broken into flight.
(Did then he share her escape, growing ecstatic wings?
Or did the sky swiftly conjure up cloud-barriers
to prevent any crazed pursuit? Do they,
transformed in new bodies, consummate a deeper love?)
He would've counted himself in her place, and who
among us foreshadowed a need for preparation?
Known but a short hour, from where they met
the air continues cracking
not solely from the onus of time
diffusing inside a heritage tea pot
but from her urgent reach back
as a last hope, before a final resignation,
till her attenuated arms lay splintered off
and he leans — paralysed in his grasping pose —
as she continues out of reach, sculpted in her destiny.

Departed, from themselves; behind them;
nobody observed.
Had the masterpiece been mislaid
it wouldn't be conjectured they were here...
among centuries, taken in an instant of violence
though now told as fantasy.
But step from her current.
Halt, to notice that fevered change of pace
which signalled earth behind them. Anchoring chains
snapped, her senses burst toward the open
to take her *immortalitas*, before she journeyed
on as one that's dead and he

was dropped, in between *here* and *there* —
a gatherer of life's emptiness.

There might've been the intervention of spirits
that inevitably look on,
beings that patrol the turbulent vacancy,
perhaps gold-mated phoenixes:
simply they were moved to migrate
once her heart had ossified.
And who
could've withstood her insensible composure
for long but them?
All delicacy of manoeuvre
those twin forms glide towards nothing for a while.
Sun-feathered and fragile,
we may be amazed how she endures
where or when they cross airless domains.
Jewelled birds, your master timed
precisely
when we lean into the unknown
too far
and cry out for wings.

(Artefacts in a display case, from matured suns modelled)
Yet, astride these ornaments, breathless, she was carried
passed-on into the miraculous,
another of the unendingly young.
Who comprehends their confinement…?
Those dew-smattered travellers, departing too soon,
who ahead of them possessed a lifetime
as if, in red, they'd signed the visitor's book?
What makes them leave so early?
What becomes of those spacious
vacant rooms almost foreseeable
their futures they never reach to occupy?
From millennia's perspective
the nameless in lengthening procession.

If you even possessed pseudonyms
against all that's unhearing night
I'd shout up to you.

Can we break with the everlasting,
stand back from fate's entrance or complain
on what's chanced in a birth-right?

Celestial horns stay calm. Such clamour is premature.
A basket of silent fruits yet performs the ceremonial part
or just one picked, at random, from a catchable branch.

Archaic craftsmen, stretching and intricately winding gold
into winged filigrees,
what does your handiwork betray:
reconnaissance of after-world reunion,
lovers' afterlife entanglement?
Too soon, inclining to the infinite, I'm appalled
how quickly life's dimensions are abandoned
for what we never have skill to design —
their long flight's incomprehension.

Overhanging all my childhood, stippled with light
one building — bolted upright at
the escarpment's edge, with a hundred thousand windows
bulged and tucked around three towers, had eyes for me.
And somewhere inside was a chamber
dedicated to lovers, lesser space
they inhabited in a crowd. But that room layer by layer
expanded, as if an arched marble grate
giving way to the fire, until criss-crossed and collapsed
at the corners, until it encompassed my whole life.
On a single afternoon, with them 'entranced'
did anyone interpret her aurora as doom?
We hardly examined...
No nuance could inform their time.

Why, with all that stretches beyond,
do we hardly dare to pre-empt it?
No matter how often our intuition predicts
the unpredictable
we refuse to act on the evidence and pretend
to leave un-guessed
the farewell assignation
or final afternoon,
rather, we prefer to sit on a strange crumbling.
That brick citadel front, I was directed not to go near,
that building greedy at noon could split its guts
and gush down the wooded slopes,
it was huge enough,
you could be caught that way. The mad stories
residents hissed about it.
That was the place fear made a start in me.
Always though, something was kept back,
you could hammer black and blue on the door.

The winter night was unfulfilled
by snow-overhanging roofs and foot-deep window ledges,
though unfinished, shimmered. From where we started,
some determined to remain behind
stood silhouetted on the fringe
against the transparent threshold.
We thought the limit further and set out to endanger
the perfect white tracing.
In those near segregated realms
harmony was at a standstill
as we stood before Your elegance
in the aspect of the never-ending.
Though scattered, each had heard announced,
there's room only for one to labour here.
Again, You detained notice and manufactured
more white crystalline, finger-carved
conclusions on tree and fence
on which we gazed astounded.

Our approach, our awkward mis-guided steps,
always we've desired to address *You*
with perfect protocol.
In our longing, unperceived was *Your* lunge towards us,
how *You* press forward to hand evidence on…as we melt away
faint with struggle, turpitude, frantic with hopelessness,
You ready us once more to confront wonder.
We meander as the Egyptian Queen
                    seeking her dead Husband
till she translates herself to a swallow
then our inaptitude's clear;
though in the legend, he remains,
by a fragment unrecovered beyond reclaiming.
You are absorbed in the Infinite.
We're primed for the second encounter…
the night, the dawn and then
the rough interiors, where we live, where childhood ceases.

Why stop and contemplate an *objet d'art* of remote epochs,
the armless Venus de Milo?
So strangely coarse appears her exposed grain-work.
For this fabrication how could an artisan have been engaged?
Are *You* also, by her supreme disaffection, over intrigued
and like us, visitors, drawn toward disappearance?
Through her has some fraction of *You* become human?
If the miraculous had never been shaped, refined,
                    never sculpted,
would we have better withstood the force
                    of our questioning?

Our position, our perpetual in-situ, is to dwell
outside an absurd universe of time and pursue entry.
At birth: to acquire the password might seem easy enough
but once, inside, towering walls
and air-tight compartments confront us.
And after our innumerable rendezvous —
sacred, profane, early, late, or kept punctually —

those engagements with time — we've still gained
no faculty to about-face, halt or leap beyond.
We only learn to quit on anguish
clinging to every small redress;
learning the coarse interior's sign,
for pain teased out
in a life's duration
that brought the torpid child to smile
and grasp the paradox of necessity.

Since, after all, the *lover* has endured his nothingness.

V

The Words

Could my word-inventions
enlighten assembled faces in earnest, with gaiety,
lifting-up a warrior's *anima* to the wind
as poets from legendary eras, ennobled
in their position after the sword and battle-axe had raged:
was death by their singing lips overcome?

When yearning's exhausted
the mind rejects all inclination
but to recede into those precincts
where no mourners wail,
gardens and woodlands which held the centre
and peacefully retreated.
Those, who loved them, ultimately
still happen to stumble across
the hidden, serpentine tracks
among the trees, and since the gate-keeper's cry is heard,
so slightly gravitate toward home:
minor edens where we belonged, where whoever
passed through left an affectionate shadow
across the continuous outlines of the earth.
Why, mother, would it hurt you to know
how many mothers there were?

You ancient praisers, joy's always desiring
to inhabit the song, still I deviate,
confused.
For us, the greatest victory was in being born,
single, or one of a multiple,
having come into the world
and imagination too unformed to resist.
You would have addressed, the dawn,
day's initial ripple of light,

for you, the first fragile sign
to herald our annunciation.

Ah, the luck of first impressions,
that column of mirrors in a department store
that never failed to return a good expression.
But I urge on forgetfulness, revoking that smiling face.
Now my privileged places
Faustian wrecking crews have demolished
a new generation capers through the glass colonnade
jaywalks across a mirror-branched Arcadia — unaware.

That feeling for 'all that was'
has been too often revived.
We know we are travelling towards.
A sight of beforehand glimmers.
Some miracle has been forecast.
There's the phenomenon of being early
a 'not yet' suspended on the horizon
(in anticipation of a new world or amor).
Yet dawn triumphs, not frenzied with expectation,
blushing from atonement, but discursive
passing-on elements of near-forgotten memories
worked-out in process:
all that means to mature, in other terms,
to communicate, fundamentally to extend across, to go
through a firmament of darkness and angle into light.
By intensity it appears night is trespassed in a single leap.
Is this our second nativity, our bewilderment — obscured
by phantoms and fantastic guardians — before the event?

Between war-steles, autocrats and the civilised,
who are we? Change is forever wrapped in the wind-god.
But if the passage, those human heroes (if slightly superior)
vanished by, had been attainable,
by which they were occluded from our vigils or wakes,
the extreme journey may've not been feared

or our quest forced toward
non-terrestrial domains:
had we continued to see them, voice-and-hand-enthralled
at their labour of song.
They frown that I dare to question
the hall of 'half-viewless harps', their absence, from where
once they began or once more are destined to return.
Some of us desire an unbroken correspondence.
Just the same, our intentions rarely resolute,
we often laugh at the futility of our libertine jests
that yet the itinerant earth continues to allow.

Ravines — secluded, night-flanked — that singers acclaim:
is that fame built isolated rock by rock through language
assigning an estranged elegance to our rapt attention?
Beside the cornice of melancholia
across the table of the agape
out from the phalanx of battle
(whatever their site of genius)
can't their words transform to reverence
lead tellurian thoughts toward the sublime?
Re-inspire us to all we have (by long-engagement)
once achieved, towards what more we could become.
Let a bardic wonder-working — as prophetic rivers
once praised — flow in and round our every instant
till our emotions, now too insipid, are flooded with fate.
Only let no answers harden.
There's space for return, room for a distant voice in our age.
Declaim unknowables, recite for us only
                      your non beginnings.

The sole testimony of the deceased: to have expanded
beyond our sentience:
no one hears the chorus of frozen trees
when they rejoice in pregnancy 'All is spring'
we glance distracted and murmur doubting words.
When spring bursts and greens the landscape

we're caught off-guard, deceived,
imagining the strength of winter, not fulfilled, but overturned
as if an avenger had risen against curlicues
of snowdrifts or iced twigs fixed in a crystalled pond.
We encumber life with delusions of triumph.
Knowledge of infinitude may guide us to an opposite lookout.
Or from the mid-zenith thunderstorm, dazzling,
some hour the orbiting earth
turns contemplative
and instructs the heart —
in the lessons of love's detachment.
Fresh from the black-overcast and reverberant after-claps
— not alone the arcing birds taste of its suffusion
but every rain-morsel moulded on the field,
a delicate faced hero looks down,
through nature's example we see how birth
could be re-composed
in the instant of dying.
(Why then do we grieve — unconscionably — the loss?)
Cloud-frontiers disperse, revealing expanses of cyan-blue,
flowers unravel to accept the urgent bees
and acres of sky plummet on distant contours,
all seems smelted, forged and hammered by a single blow
such an artefact rumbles underfoot —
still the earth, still the vast green spin.

To be healed, to be made whole:
the dawn, that immaculate of light,
can't be prescribed.
Though we arrive early in a noble gesture of grief
like those who discovered the entrance-stone removed,
Iris hardly glimmers with pinks and mauves
before it bows to the strengthening form
behind thread-loose colours,
in no time consumed
in the sun's life-ward surge.

On the margin of a mid-autumn acre of sunflowers,
daylight diminishing, I find myself rejoicing in their existence.

Those followers and buds of the sun
so heavy with age and drooping,
what runs your course down to malaise
whilst the seed-kernels ripen?
You shake your hearts open, overturning
the proudest stem's support.
I watch them writhing in unbearable fatness
as if martyrs contorted in fire.
You desert the earth to be
as immense, as high in expansive space, as majestic;
to touch the sun's rooted in them
and because you advance close —
closer than any can envisage —
they're burned back, levelled to dust,
as if overwhelmed by your own passion.

In human relations, life's withdrawing sigh
often passes unnoticed.
A too frantic sense of injustice impedes our listening.
Allow me to carry a sadness for what I've never known
whose absence
I can never understand.
Could we accept this refined separation
their ripeness, their transparency
given-up in the sun's presence?
On occasion old praisers help to tell
though it would leave us rooted in despondency
to know: how uninvolved we are.

VI

Mother — Father

Through tempest of birth, no language utters
a mother's desire-despair. Only a translatable
between spasms of an interpreter that speaks
          and then goes mute
as though fighting for breath, announces once more:

Sting no more that you wait
come through as you will to be
I will receive you.

Subdue terror of first impression
this is still the passionate earth, my vast green planet.
In one night made visible —
full of nourishment —
still overrun with elegance and wonder
perfectly gripped in orbit and turned on its axis,
still the living earth,
no one can throw suffocating arms around.

Within her body, an outraged double,
with a language (only deciphered) replies:

O don't let me go round too fast
      for once
we're not born
for you or yours,
we come into the world
to assume the unknown,
we're born to ride shreds of black wind
from an invisible horse's mane
we come fable-legged and matched of face
shiny with speed of entry.

Call us down   we arrive in suffering.
Think open space gone   we come despite it.
We rush through the tempest of stomping feet
tight feelings break
we snap up the first whim of sky and earth
left unprotected, we make it ours
your demand made:
'Sting no more   that you wait!'

All at once, language desists.
Voice undeterred
sprays from the veil
as a waterfall giving off mist
and we stand drenched
in that greater nearness of the still-to-be-born:
those far, precariously advanced,
who've evolved to the least tenable limit,
trembling, in readiness, at the verge of new existence —
appear as primordial lives or remotest star-flames —
before assuming their human form
with the out-cry of life-desire.
In being born, we're taken by a fit of possession
as if from the head waters we were conceived.
And we must, once given life, remain true to the unborn
as to you, mother; if we saw you as alone
you'd become no more than the gap in the infinite-scape,
through which the mass of beings, ourselves, tumbles,
no more than a barren gateway, unaffected.
But we sense how much you are affected
and feel thighs being eroded, as a river bank
how you lose to our current as we rage into being.
But with all that seems prefigured
you demand an actual affinity
desire a prolonged alliance.
And we react, taking on that position
suffering with you — a response, secretly yearned.
So, at our prime inhalation,

in urgency of becoming human,
we yet cry out and hear how you —
awaking from your own death
in sudden recovery — call *My child. My child.*
When first our breath bores through the film of endless
  sleep your claim of life-giver is indisputable.

But before:
we were strangers to your skin,
and late in you
we couldn't be sustained,
with mixed loyalties
we leaped
to be early in him, in *patra*, in father.

Yet, father, don't celebrate too much
we were enough in-sickened-love to suckle from her.
A night-lamp guest,
a magician's entry
the sexual act
that's all the admittance required to steal
into the glare of day
and peer at you, magnifying
every crease, blemish and blotch of your mountainous face.

Afterwards, we don't inspect faces we encounter
not with that same intensity.
Faces stare, when they detect us watching in lapsed moment,
at those kindest conjunctions
a returning glance can chase us deep into ourselves,
especially that cast of an angry father,
in his expression, as if through a mask, the world stares.

From remote regions, from further mythology,
equine daughters, she-riders of the north,
wore your visage pressed to divine disobedience.
They trusted so heavily in fatherlove.

But you could never take them back; thus your violence.
An image lies pregnant in you a lifetime.
From high crags, so rigid browed,
instead, you pronounce judgement.
Our praise of your vast panorama
falters, nullified by terror.
On you, how you cast that gaze, so much depends.
From us to scale impossible peaks seems demanded.
Through each sweat-exhausting dream-typology
we belong to you — from that ritualised location
you never can honour *difference*
and abandon separation to us,
where we, treacherously, begin and you at last leave off.

Finally across heaven and earth, make true the bridge
between us, father. Let us
throw arms around each other's shoulders,
brought to joined love through pain's shared duration.

But, always, our environment's abstract.
I perceive you now further away than ever
beyond life's circumference controlling me
through your greater estrangement
and more unflinching defiance.

Yet, among unreliables
a part of me, I hunt for you:
the one prejudiced against,
gone from my youth, untrusted, an alien.

Again, the vision of your head returned
then is submerged once more
below memory and feeling, overwhelmed
by gushing waters, by the image of horses
with black slick flanks, rumbling between columns:
one word's roar comes from the mouth of the riders
'Disowned!   Disowned!'

VII

Another Country's Hills

It seems I abandoned my younger brother, Stephen,
by the bedroom window scared at the yellow moon's stare
and said under breath 'it's his battle, I can't fight it';
left him and travelled across an ocean
in search of my name.

It seems summer overtook me
and re-made me as winter.
The pure yellow march of sun
passed by and for an age
I loved that inhuman embrace.

It was only right the elements should have their play.
Did we not come? Look, they puzzle what brought us on
to the field's seat, at the wind's steering
to face that which is best perhaps never to face
the stone blue skylark or albatross
ocean or sky's domain.

And our sight betrays, as an eye of a needle
not to see but to be seen is sacred.

I praise the simple gifts,
all that comes about as given
handed on once more from what has always been
reconceived through generations.
I remember
a scene inherited, an old sculptor's workshop
and under his creative grip and wink
inspired statues were given voice
'from the start we've built you
in your blood we've always been.'
To sustain this seems all that was required.

Go tough in your course —
but who can be a rebel in the veins?
Or how can it be withheld from conscience
if a site of Parnassus is here —
years from now I'll claim sanctuary for
                    your crumpled work-boots.

Grandpa, my feet always ran, whilst you limped.
You had a curse of a job to make your lousy feet shift.
When you transfixed a tree with your artist's intent
you stood off-balance, lop-sided.
Our delicate world swiftly collapsed
under immeasurable years that were somehow counted.
When time came to leave, just my walking away, could erode.
One hand's always bent on fleeing from the other.
Quick, that hopeless anguish of authorship, of origins, if I could
I would forgo — birth-blemishes of the yearning to create —
as if a tongue-out against the elusive Olympians
a denying of the womb. You were always the master.
Your piano, too, in the hall, invited virtuosos to perform.
Us they must scorn now
our rash insistence on perfection.

Observe: like a magician's stunt,
fresh from winter
into the absence of spring —
the early iris like a flame wet and green.

I could stay in this field forever.
Dare you, was tossed back
by the one with him that day,
as if a learned, well grounded, no —
and yet, new, the wish never imagined before.

Who calls that fleet bird from the styled heavens?
Passive on the dry rocks, it shares in the stonewalls.
Though soaring to finality, it shifts the patterns

conferred on flight,
stripping the layers, till down like an arrow's tip
until further down, covered by flesh of earth.
Once, out of line, without background,
fallen, near vanishing —
so enduring to the mind to perfect this,
                    refining to the emotions.

On mid-ocean
what single form flew
beside our steel hulk
unalerted by landlessness?

What airborne scout prior to light
rested and guided along the deserted sea
with a beat and hum of wings?

For those who've sighted such phenomena
no fire-torturing tongs were needed —
only the heart's warmth held in the grip of forgiveness.

Have it be, let it come into being,
don't look stunned and beg for a reprieve
against the power of that calm to transform us.
As we rose through you
we grew out of you.
A storyteller awakes confinement
for one child, a playhouse, another, a cage;
the home seed ignited
and about us the great world as a bubble. All was not well.
A sand castle's anger stirred.
Invisibles were commanded to appear
becoming our earliest dolls.

Their balloon eyes must burst.

Here and now it serves us —
a frank desperation to escape.
I must touch your solid head
without being knobbly fingered
and near ruined by innocence
as if all things were offered as unreachable.

Wide world, this is our turn,
no other destination, as much
as in steps of pilgrims, one foot in front of the other.
Ahead, mountains and valleys extend.
Inspired in their own manner;
back to their beginnings we cannot force them:
rain soaked with houses, walls and trees,
they don't slip or topple,
a saturated night-land,
not bumps on skin
but another country's hills, as if each
set aglow by the bottom-most coals.

Let the lack of reflection influence
and being refused mirrors, the miles
may thicken like honey:
this, only this, no more than to journey.

Which of you would call us back too soon
and rest the strange landscape untried?
The Snow Queen they went out by
and back through a snowflake they arrived.
If you see us as failures on our way home,
how did you greet them?
Quieter than us they sit: their tale's recovery,
landed on your doorstep, dressed for reappearance.
                    Still, you notice
they don't follow your adoring eyes as they did once
because wiled away in your look of disbelief

was that which by inches matured
and was understood, their leg heavy miles in between.
Those who kept with them, amassed
unasked-for seasons: summer changed to blue
turned pink, crystallised, long before autumn.
Might it happen, though, that we reach round a sharp corner,
tunnel through
or are hoisted over the wall,
at the next kingdom's reversal,
we might, suddenly, be shocked to catch them
in the bare leap of becoming.

Was that
what I longed for
from you?

Dear dead man,
between your persona, unageing,
and me, what is love?
A journey never to be fulfilled?

Nature's not as we would have
what there is, it proclaims:
in a foreign field the skylark's firmly lodged.
At a ship's bite the radiant spray
chisels no surface,
inches deep, as fathomless,
about us an undisturbable blue surrounds..

As closer the shore draws
it implies no bereavement.
Land and sea grow undivided
as if never allowing a gap for a bridge to be swung.

Look,
ahead, beyond the curved bow, an emblem of land.
I turn to my fellow passenger, an aged Stephen,

expecting confirmation; but after an unbroken pause
he says, *there's an image for a voice
that continues without echo.*

Earth, this dust-fine love and oldness,
always whole, always wandering, like glass.

Finding a Blue Door in Oxford

Day one, I stroll the right-a-way shadowing the once frantic towpath to Iffley. Nothing underfoot of the hoof-marks of yoked horses hauling barges. From the green bank boats idle, waiting their captains. The river slumbers under a mist-veil, before a summer's day breaks.

reflected
in the Thames, one prow
reads *Gypsy Scholar*

from sedge a lark's
cry... mingles with
a coxswain's *Row! Row!*

buried in summer
a wrecked bench — a place
damselflies repose.

Underneath a vandalised signpost, designed to direct tourists,
after a snatched conversation

a retired craftsman's
right hand quivers toward
the Norman church

The door's locked. I admire the Romanesque façade, meander through a hare bell graveyard. Saturday, so the organist arrives to practise and I'm allowed in. The narrow interior has three column-divided sections, three emblematic steps towards the altar. After a while, restraining his fugues, he explains the building's character, pointing to a recent bequest, a baptismal window. As he illuminates, I listen to blues in John Piper's stained-glass, his summer sky-blues.

Iffley village with vistas, a view to the weir-pond and lock has been preserved: a tunnel-vision between high walls. I'm inclined to sit on a perched bench, gaze and ruminate, but walk by.

Early afternoon, returning to Oxford, heat overwhelms, I pay and enter the 17th century Botanic Gardens, partially enclosed by pinnacled towers and scripted façades of the University colleges. On the quarter hour, listen to separate bells chime like hearing debates of Christology as between time. First, Christ Church's spire, discoursing bell to bell, then Magdalene retorts.

After trudging raddled gravelly walks, examining with fading interest the flora's exotic names and attitudes of sculpture, or marvelling at antics of punters in the tributary, I collapse spread-eagled in the brief shade of a Latinised tree and observe the fantastic forms of the sun's topiary.

Later, heat receding, I begin sight-seeing again, past foregrounds of the Radcliffe Camera and Bodleian Library, where black-gowned graduates link arms for group photographs. I eavesdrop on a guide's survey of the architecture. He changes, a ventriloquist, one language to the next; describes age and significance. Entering St. Mary's, University cathedral, in a meditative choir I encounter, for less than a second, history. Englishness inhabits this site of trials of conscience, peace and religious suffering. In casual garments, Madrigal Singers, in the nave, rehearse for an evening concert, a medieval sound-cloth for me and other sightseers. Some, previewing the recital, sit in pews. The head singer addresses his fellow artists at times with 'No that won't do...let's try again'. I explore the Church — a gift shop bars the main entrance with hard-sell-tactics and votives. In the choir a bank of candles flickers speechless like a miniature wood.

The vaulted site, hung with Renaissance art, expands, cluttered with heritage. Its decor is history in stone; incongruities in an eccentric design. John and Charles Wesley preached here and John Henry Newman declared controversies, teaching the need for a seraphic

Church. Nothing, between historiated walls, grew as a tree in an arbour. Faiths, theories and convictions, were cut-off requiring centuries to be re-grafted, or lost in clamour of immediate judgements. No suspended proclamations or worded doubts confront, but the emptiness of a place that can't be re-occupied: evidence that a conservator knows, eludes rescue. I scan remnants, hollows on a stone tomb-lid that fine brass inlaid, or a plaque to martyrs of Queen Mary — fastened crudely to a pillar. I read how a creed first recanted was followed by a second unearthly affirming. Between politics and religious cult, a slenderest parting exists where a provocative act, perhaps a love-act breathes: as if Thomas Crammer's first finger trembles already toward the fire's flesh.

The day ends observing at the back of my guesthouse: small, unripe apples through indigo.

On the second day, tempted to skirt Oxford's core and disappear to the parkland on the apron, I resist. Elaborate finials, corbels, oriel windows project from colleges. Mosaic faces on pillars around the Sheldonian Theatre, in morning brightness, carry emotive overtones. Revelation or restfulness? Forecourts of hectic activities subdued, cobbles glow as curved backs of fish. Shadows zigzag through a street's heart or scar the dusty complexion of archaic buildings. Unhurrying, not lost, uncertain where I am to the map now and then consulted, I see a middle-aged, Sunday-suited gentleman gazing at fabulous profiles. I close in, he turns to address me. I expect a hesitant note of amazement. *All in all I prefer Cambridge slightly to Oxford*, he informs. I say nothing. He's not my guide. Half pleased stroll by niches full or void.

My visit has this analogy. I'd gaze through scrolls of a wrought-iron gate, watch an advantaged world idle, play serious, light-hearted games. In return, it might show a glimpse. Down a shadowed, arched portico I'd see two fellows confer, a quad observed, decorative with rose, wisteria or ivy, a pampered stretch of lawn leads to famous steps, a terrace revealed. Then, unexpectedly (certainly I'd be deceived) that élite domain vanishes and grimaces like a gargoyle with indifference, grins as mouldings of irony. It disappears behind landmarks and gate-closing-times. It doesn't matter if I wear a gown, pay for photographs or access, obey rules. Once attracted it closes-up pretends it has never been open to explore. Expertise we learn in childhood games such as hide and seek would not help us gain entry. That world puffs-away. Too proud to be a tourist. Earth, under-shoe, I deem mine. Don't care whose blood seal impresses. I can't excuse dreaming spires that forget the humility out of which they were born.

silly white jasmine
blossoming on vulgar walls
now I see your tact.

Resolving conflicts, I leave etiquette and exquisite facades. Parkland is simple to find. Sense a connection between green environs and the city's authority whose overlooking townscape outline the parks. Walter Benjamin says, documents of civilisation and barbarism are closely related. I'm willing to hair-split the distinction with each step as I reach the entrance.

once through the kiss-gate —
fragrance of evergreen!

Decay in the woods, crumbling, feeling of abandonment, ethos of loss combines with return. In the open a tree hams it up, not performing as it should at this year's quarter in this climate:

thin, dying birch
can't cast enough shade
for a butterfly.

Shade's a consideration after my ear-scorching yesterday. Under the umbrella of a poplar I fix myself to a bench, close to the main walkway. A concourse of Sunday strollers and explorers gradually pass. Rough-riders. Three boys race on mountain bikes. The leader drops something white like a pair of underpants (may be they've been swimming in the river). The following boys stop by the object screaming ahead to the first, who halts and straddles his bike. *You dropped something,* one of the followers shouts. *And look! it's got something brown on it.* The duo yell in mock disgust. Then climb on their bikes and speed to the first youngster who doesn't return and retrieve what's been dropped. Instead, they zoom off together. What he will say when he gets home, or will it matter? How explain away his carelessness or won't it be noticed? Is he already conjuring a cover-up? In any case, his damp underpants lay elementally stained. Unnoticing, three different aged women come past, well acquainted, discussing episodes from the workweek. One says, *They usually ignore each other. Yes, I never see the two of them together* another woman seconds. *But over this issue...*a third begins. Her words disappear in the breeze or turn into birds. I lose a sentence picking up the close ... *they're jealous.* The three women walk on, topic shifting, discuss the care and supervision of parents. I hear a voice through the trees by the riverbank, calling with no inflection of danger.

Toby come here! Now...........Toobbyy!
the wind intervenes.

Occupy this seat. In a few minutes the sun will climb over the poplar and transform with down-pouring rays. Stay, thinking how once I experienced such transformation, how a bright attribute lingered behind a leaf-screen — my vague emotions — then appeared blinding and couldn't be shunned. Something secluded, with fragile lineaments, then exposed, could no longer be hidden, was burned to ash. Discovery and concealment play-the-goat, until shock at the hope or grief attached overpowers us. Who overcomes this dark-light struggle?

Don't propose grey-merging. Sometimes a feeling emerges that withstands its discovery. Platonic or erotic, joint representatives, I contemplate love. What's the best tactic? When outcome matters, we play to win. Do episodes exist, unplanned careless, when we perform?

the sun spotlights
a couple's entwining kiss
she on tip-toes.

The observation can be read as sexist. Don't claim this portrait's the sole reality within my sight. Could draw the two figures in diverse ways, that wouldn't suggest she looks up to him as a superior. I mean physical stature. Her gesture can indicate a greater enthusiasm, sincerity or power than his passive height implies like the city's tall spires. Many interpretations are possible. The image is a surface. Another twosome step into view, teenagers out for a stroll, a quarrel strides between; too distant from each other. She says, *Why ya in a mood with me?* He replies, throwing a bag he's been carrying at her feet. She responds, hurling loose change at his. A child either attached or a stranger comes up and kicks the few glinting coins which inspires a smile from her; he remains stalwart in his scowl. I leave them and walk beside the Cherwell, observing the gesticulation of grasses rooted in the stream's sandy bottom.

did once movement
of fish rule the fate of love
in these shallows too?

she strokes his red ear
he shuns her invitation
playing 'the hard man'.

lovers' reflections
toss into stillest water
tentative pebbles.

between her and him
she builds a Milky Way —
at last he offers a star.

Above a haze of forget-me-nots I can see them. Reconciliation's comforting and healing for a collective or personal historette. I fear someday he will beg, fight for *rapprochement*. Amnesty will be withheld that this hour gives. 'Man!' I want to holler, 'throw off that false hauteur while it's a tee-shirt before it's your second skin!' I feel a voyeur, it's time to move. I remember my follies, loves, 'fatuations (if there's such a word). Illusions, like the debris in black sacks, heaped on a tractor-pulled trailer that now lumbers by; the scattered park bins emptied. The driver masks a frown on her juvenescent face. For the young (statistics claim) disappointment is dangerous. Those nearest to make-believe are closest to forced departure, ready to fling themselves, cut unruckled wrists or swallow chemical pearls. An attractive nuance surrounds self-conviction, as if leaving life cradles a promise of freedom, escape from physical pain, weakness, age's generic sorrows and separations I've known since adolescence, written in tomes and minds. As well, avoid later embarrassments of recurrent teenage longing.

fresh green seduces...
someone endeared turns their back
on the world again

Tilted against vanish-ment is the wisdom of a Blue Door (not H. G. Wells' deceptive green door hiding eternals) but the front door that an elderly man painted painstakingly, on the last day of life. He didn't rule time to assess workmanship, receive praise or envy of neighbours. Visualise him, with a blue-doused brush, stroking rectangular panels with rhythmic precision, dabbing corners of moulding, oblivious to imminent death, interested in his fate. The door, since then, has been re-coated three, four times, thrown away and a new-styled entrance hung or the house demolished, with bits and pieces scattered or jutting from the ground. Why does his act of painting a door blue counter suicide, if diligence can't prevent destruction? Not by evidence of being insensible, but the way he tends to a small portion, performing a sub-plot with verve in the face of the main-storyline. A sign of a human perspective. His disproportionate concern gives more meaning to the small than to greatness, reversing perceived valuation. To kill oneself and leap into night is a gesture of the gods, to go on caring for matters of transient notoriety, despite the end's intimacy, implies an earthly conscience. The blue door a human-scaled artefact a museum can't display, store, or appear as an endnote in historiography. If recorded, it stands a backdrop to a family picture, either mounted among hundreds or discolouring in a drawer, otherwise the blue door's history is here, in my mind.

stray bristles
on the upright blue plane
quick-brush-flicks free

Standing, stretching, kneeling, crouching, he proceeds: preparation, under-coat, gloss. (Three days' work). Liberality, Temperance, Magnificence. (In different orders depending on mood and circumstance). To a medieval cleric, painting the door, might've been deficient, when prayer and vigil better ready one for infinite night. To an Epicurean the task would've appeared too isolating for each moment's social urgency. The act is not solely functional, repeating an ethic, since it achieves magnificence. He defies burdened evidence of the meaningless, to create, not a new life. Soon as the performance concludes the ideal he conceives, is vanishing. Freshly coated entrance is not his infant. Ornamentation on Iffley's façade, a more just comparison, if remembered his action isn't intended to symbolise permanence or display worship. Marvel at Sunday amblers and show-offs, on serpentine paths, picnickers in shadows of columnar trees. Watch them shun the over-hanging immensity to practise noon hour ceremonies and relaxations. They imitate an advanced species but I suspect if they perceived the onus of the impassable distance under which they appear to reside, the knowledge would grind them to fragments smaller than irregular stones under the *pad, pad, pad* of a joggers' steps? Then overhead, everyday mallards glissade with rigid wings.

helter-skelter above the grass
miniature plane or dragonfly

a chestnut sweeps the blue
with Van Gogh's brush

in and out of shade picnickers
examine truths among Pied Beauty.

Walking to Magdalene Bridge, I climb its arc, find a vantage. At this height, 'dreaming spires' come in view: marketers' caption to subtitle a brochure. The epithet diffuses meaning and ironic potential. I lean from a small platform. From here, a friend's reported, students leap in celebration of their finals' end. Here too, intoxicated or euphoric, some throw themselves and expect to splash, soaked stagger ashore; instead sometimes are snapped-up from life through chaotic gaiety of the carnivalesque. Loving abandoners deserve crepe arm bands. The towers hemming us with murals, architraves and chiselled cusps never dress in delirious mood.

Should we weep with equal sorrow, if they crumble to a heap of broken images? From this scenic view, dreams contest: one, styled abandonment, tends to destruction, the other, aspiring, turns ambitious, inclines to cruelty. They stand a few yards apart, feign abuse from rival teams. Between contestants, what humour or sense of honour endures? Interrupting two teenage cyclists with plaid shirt-tails fluttering, fly across the bridge forgetting gravity.

I answer: the poetic, creative ideal exists; others, suspending judgement, share. Yet an artist's accomplishment can be misread or lost. How does a novelist or poet fall from favour? Through misconduct or by a status erected that pays homage warning of the danger of acclaim? Can't comprehend what it means that someone's work or person, held in high esteem, falls.

Past assessments look naive. The present, second to second, appears to even up truth and fiction. On balance, too, opinions develop (we guess) toward moral, intellectual clarity and synthesis. But the past, by some, stands preferred. They ignore, yesterday was once a broken up here and now, had its own imagined confluence, an envisioned tomorrow that with time's passing became nothing but our own disparate present. All we can safely announce is change.

Styles of tolerance alter. We dread to admit a line, perfect image, idolised in text or love relationship can deteriorate until unreadable. Yet, I distrust change, expressed in adolescent leaps and reversals, as distrust the continuum of pinnacles. Who ride rocking-horses of fashion against sublime hardened edifices? I feel for a middle ground. And yet, on that meridian who keeps balance for long, before an in-turned passion or grievance, tips them over into prejudice? The university landscape urges me to recall that T.S. Eliot negotiated the flux and ebbs, skirted protruding rocks, unexpected shallows, now and then capsizing: boatmanship that shows a fallible writer's search and skill before the world, fame, before The Waste Land.

beneath Magdalene Bridge
some ridiculous, some skilled —
brave punters poling.

For fallen creators let's preserve signs of defeat, a crack across a window, a shooting star's path crystallised into an eternal needle-line. Imagine looking up at trajectories of the fallen. A pick-up-sticks of light. Dome of space scratched with irremovable routes of disgraced fates. Was this what Greek astronomy was about? Or carve initials in a collapsed trunk disturbing river-traffic for a century. Spots for star-gazing or tree-caressing, guarded like famous monuments; nadirs for the everyday to reflect on the summits from which the great tumble. I anticipate this high-arching bridge's peak is a remembrance site for some, closing my eyelids.

under my feet
the raised path vibrates...
like violin strings

I've practised for years the art of pretending to be blind, to regain sensitivity. Shut my eyes tight and try not slip off the kerb, crash into a wall or streetlight pole. Often I open *my windows-to-the-soul* too soon. Time becomes infinite, fatigue overtakes when usual markers vanish. Can't measure time without knowledge of distance between things. Can't internalise. Whatever's meant by a body clock, must demand discipline for a person with impaired sight to master time until an instinct. I tear the hood of darkness off to visualise what leads ahead, because of a naked longing to see a nominal future, if illusory. In artificial nights all becomes past or intense presence. Every step I venture is a battle between my will and the will of light.

My blind-man's bluff is a game daring the sun. I can't imagine the absence of sight. Can I feel celebration that pushes someone to jump into blind water or that despair? I sense the disappointment that awaits. To spring from the historic edge over a wrought barrier is trying to escape boundaries which still encircle the leap into space. It's mortifying we can't dodge them. Poetic sages proclaim: the margins encompass no alien parterre or exclusion zone, but this world. Accustomed space and ground surrounds reveller or meditator, midnight or noon, a dive in joy or anguish: that world we could forgive and love at the moment our sight ends.

On the third day, I set out to explore further the sensuous familiar Thames. Its water burning from sun-shafts, names of tied-up boats melt in passing wakes. Before half a mile, exhausted I collapse on a sycamore-shaded bench. Without an introduction a robin perches. Start conversing with it, looking into, with its gold corolla, its dark solar eye that doesn't reflect mine as if the eye Odin plucked from his face to gain wisdom. Interrupted by heavy sparse words and scraping boot-tough soles I see five coarse youngish men homing in on my bench.

Two sit close and three take up positions, standing in front. They're applying some kind of pressure. I'm unclear what they want. The strongest who seems the leader sits one away. Sweating, he has a cold beardy face, but doesn't look as threatening as the quick-aging teenager standing middle with a hard stare like a concealed knife. The group begins a loose conversation, pretending to be oblivious as if I occupied a favourite riverside perch and would take the hint moving on at a moment's notice. The leader unsatisfied with the tactic, butts in, catching my worried eyes, and repeats: *It's too hot.* They want a drink? They carry dusty denim-jackets as limp hyssop sacks over shoulders. Their jeans over-worn, tee-shirts falling to bits match their stance. The possible thugs might be linked in intrinsic ways: a raiding party. I question if they slept together along the river last night or have left plush residences on a morning scrounge. Don't linger on speculations. Keep trying to engage them in an everyday semi poetic language, pretending nothing strange is happening, to fend off whatever's their message. For a second the pressure turns extreme; the leader searches my eyes, every part for an answer to who I am, vulnerable or not, someone to respect or torment. I fail to grasp their purpose entirely and they can't decide on what to demand and in which way to enforce it.

The blue door, still wet. If blossoms — apple, ornamental cherry, pear or wisteria, fall, measling panels, what would the craftsman do? Would frustration ruin him? Try to remove tissue petals with authoritative dips to restore the surface to absolute blue? He might include the chaotic fall in his design; bond flower-swish and sweep of brush-strokes, accept imperfection as part of his perfect scheme as if a blue-dipped paintbrush could dance on its own off the ground.

The five have landed from clouds, taken on earth-covers, dirty and haggard, by chance or design. They look unsure if I'm a touring god dipping down from heaven. I'm dressed a visitor. After a pause, the headman scrutinises. I wish he'd command I empty my pockets, strip off. What do they want money or blood? I would know; the brain-searching would stop.

He gives an un-cruel glance, a bit-off smile; with an outburst of energy rises to his feet. No scowl of grief, disgust, disappointment, he accepts I haven't got the message and time's up. He silently addresses his cohorts. The group starts along the old towpath, troops in a rag-tag appearance, or seeking a better victim. Throw salutations over their shoulders. Leave with: *have a good stay... hope you enjoy the city... maybe we'll see you in Oxford again sometime.*

mute swans
move and don't move
the space between

York Memories

A Morning Visit To My Estranged Wife During Her Severe Illness

I
At home: her proud head
lolling on purple cushions;
a pink dressing-gown cries out.

II
Outside, round droplets
on a clothesline won't hint at —
her long anguished night.

III
She clambers — steps squeak —
what she calls her marathon.
Coming down she dreads.

IV
Two abstract swallows
on a grey vase — support white
of valley lilies.

V
She crawls to breathe-in
flowers that have lost their scent, except
for one who loves them.

Early March Serial

To Arthur Benson, past folk curator at the Castle Museum, York
who revealed the intimacies of historical facts.

My life sign has been the moon. Passing fifty, I meet change differently than at twenty. I reminisce, forget and re-shape, approach the vanishing present looking back.

whole moon tonight.
more than a silver face,
I meet living grimaces…

A Man of Letters who's eclipsed his eightieth birthday. Attend his poetry reading in a hard-chair hall; he ends with more 'rarefied obscure' words, — that have been selected for publication by Ted Hughes (he says). He claims that one poem (if you listen) sounds like a blackbird's song. A short symposium followed. Afterwards, washing my hands in the gent's basin, I hear the voice of his disguised suffering rise from a toilet cubicle.

over a white bowl,
not banquet-engorged or drunk
a poet-scholar heaves.

My way home, I pass, on light-fickle pavement, a never seen again itinerant, who greets with a prudish face and quicksilver smirk, as if I must be glad to make his acquiesce.

a homeless zigzags
to a shelter, muttering
in time … in time.

Mrs. Ward twenty years has grieved for a husband, childless marriage. Pause by her door. Drapes drawn in a closed face. Past midnight ponder how promise and mischance joined to lead her to isolation. No chance, this hour, to knock and see how she is.

edging dark soil
gold crocus nearly disclose
a widow's despair.

Two days later I'm a museum attendant, watching visitors through the gallery: children awe-struck, bored or 'wasted' teenagers in school parties with question-sheets, or meandering adults, alone or in twos. They peer into glass-cases, stare over wooden barriers into reconstructed rooms. I overhear them: *I remember that… It's just like home or I can't believe people once lived like this*, and the proverbial inquiry an attendant must endure: *Is he alive?*

Sometimes a visitor extends his or her fingers toward me, but mostly over the barrier, trying to touch or lure an artefact — empathy or devilment — setting off alarms. Whatever the commotion at the corridor's far end the museum's arcane work continues…

through a coded door
conservators clean, re-join
unstable objects.

Also, part of my chores, I care for *things*, museum pieces, beyond the status of memorabilia. In an exhibit entitled 'Every Home Should Have One' cleaning with a miniature brush around a rusted turn-table like a god's discus, I heard scratchy rhythms.

black record fragments
in a twenties' gramophone
sing *love's forever*.

After work, a perpetual walker, I take an old route, forgotten alongside the way routinely followed. This light-lingering afternoon, stroll among dissimilar markers.

lion-loping clouds cross
his still open-drapes bay-window
through dismembered blue.

George L. Simms lived here, a widower who after reprieves died without warning. He believed he was clairvoyant. In his Phil Larkin semi instructed with stories about his spiritual guardian Red Cloud he first met in the 1930s. The spirit said it would soon return, re-materializing in the 50s. I thought Red Cloud unlikely name for a Yorkshire ghost, but George didn't comment. I never disputed. With blue eyes set in his pocked face, he puzzled on Red Cloud's delay, why earthly and spiritual time didn't coincide.

has his genii moved?
who never failed to welcome
bow to my compeer.

George insisting on an extra world, was devoted to this. *It's a honour to attend to small creation, a pleasure to exist, fulfilling rescued by the unknown. To take responsibility for everything, blaming no one, he said, leaves a sweet taste in your mouth.*

with second sight
he coaxed dawn-chorus thrushes:
breadcrumbs to thousands.

his lop-sided birdbath
improvised from a dust bin lid
gleams with rainwater.

He trusted occult experiences. Speaking to his grieving wife about their diphtheria-lost nine year old, he'd said. *I spoke to Ruth last night; from the other side she assured me there was no cause to mourn.* More earth-bound than George I visualise...

on a fence briefly
through nor-westerly moans
a titmouse perches.

One mood of March turns inward, a meditation on the end, another stretches to welcome spring's arrival. Once attentive, gazing, a fur-coated passer-by quipped, *Don't do it.* I kept my stance, believing reflection more creative than suicidal. In late evening, by a barb-knotted fence, my wind-breaker zipped, stained brown hiking-boots carry me by:

haphazard snowdrops
guarding a rubbish mound
with night closed petals

I remember Mrs. O'Callaghan, a dedicated nurse, who cared for her infirm mother whom she felt, no matter her efforts and attention that she was somehow neglecting.

flustered chrysants:
(at noon yesterday) once more
relaying her haste.

among fleeting thought
an old mansion unfolds
with dew on its sills

A generation ago: myself, two husbands, two wives (dual babies) we laboured to make an honest thoughtful life — resembling a Samuel Coleridge Pantisocracy. We pledged to care for 'un-abled' adults estranged from their own families. Two black Labradors heeled as sentinels by the babies' prams as if the new-borns were destined to be closest friends. We worked on, restoring the garden's tangled legacy, the pine-framed estate and stone tall-windowed house, cutting ingrown ivy, knocking down loose plaster, re-painting. One night a bucket tilted; water cascaded down the out-dated stairs. We laughed. Another day the estate's last gardener came smashing through undergrowth to walk old paths. For a time we shared our psychic-space in a nearby cottage. After a struggling winter, moved into the big, partly refurbished house — here and there a floor board missing — we needed to be cautious when finding our bedrooms after night dialogues tailed off and the next day's urgency breached our consciousness.

five true freethinkers
crossed a threshold — years ago —
against unknown doors.

In angry outbursts, divorce, accusations, a utopian scheme, our cherished project unravelled. We few fabled first arrivants were forced to disperse, some fated never to meet again. The thrashing toward a honest and loving existence is carried on by other co-workers (we were coined) less idealistic, more compromising with experience to back them up, and carried on by the residents — disabled or 'otherly abled' or 'challenged' in current usage, kind hapless beings sent to redeem our ambitions. I recall the flower blush on two women's cheeks and strength in young men's eyes on that March day we moved in; after hardship came achievement and ease. A promised renewal filled the forsythia air, its fragrance swept through the heaviest doors.

The next day, I'm back in the museum: on duty in my blue shirt-trouser uniform. (A little anti-deodorant at dawn). Between giving directions, seeking lost children, between lunch and tea breaks, I ruminate on how, personal or universal, history's uncovered and re-buried between instants of evidence. Tourists from around the world pass alongside the restored artefacts — one headlines his blue baseball cap with USS Arizona.

room of icons:
the Georgian clock
pauses to reflect.

Some days it isn't easy to restore: cleaning a glued together Japanese vase with plum blossom design can be hard to handle and if you use the wrong cleaning solution the vase might re-fracture; the fixative could be water-based (unlike Basho's helmet there's no cricket underneath to add a final irony) Or you might rub a brass badge on an antique convertible until the special date and name on the bonnet disappears — the very reason for the vintage car to be exhibited. Tending to provenance requires a delicate touch:

white gloved fingers
lead meditative dial-hands
back to here and now.

The everyday world under a few stars feels like a museum, imitating a remoter reality. The next late winter dawn, not walking, I stand at a bus shelter and encounter mimesis in the form of a flushed, young woman. She's fled disaster, worked late at a nightclub, just left her lover's side or reeled from a narrow bed after a bad dream. She's not at peace or dressed for this early appointment with public transport, a work day's demanding haste. There's no queue, only me to witness her marooned appearance.

boarding, walking to
the back — I can't face dawn's light
in love-fragile eyes.

The passenger sits passive as a once lost artefact exuding time. Then, *sub silentio*, at another empty stop, the bus doors fold back, and as if a perfumed figurine had gained legs, she disappears carrying her distress, unrequited love and endless hopes with her.

a fading moon taunts,
How passé... to wish ...
my crazed admirer.

lumbering along
untold signs of re-birth, no
side-plot without green.

Arriving, uniform under my Mac, like someone coming to a masquerade ball, I stroll over the museum's threshold, past Doric columns — written with first beams. Little idea how the day might turn out. Inside, in the lobby I greet the shiny 19th century red and brass fire engine, a tested friend, say *Good morning* to the head attendant steaming to some task with black shoes clicking. Later, across the same tiles, Arthur Benson will lead a children's school group to show them favourite curiosities from the past. Strange, we humans spend much time and energy gazing in the rear view, reconstructing yesterday, when we can't go back to one of its places or reuse one of its things — except to value them as souvenirs of the lost. What era is it, between then and now, when vinyl fragments in a rusted gramophone sing *love's forever*?

The Old Boer War Monument

Standing at ease in storm-weathered granite
eight soldiers keep an un-war-like-watch
on the civilian crowds that hurry across
Duncombe Place. In this season, under
the varied uniform stone combatants,
some of the open green lies fenced off
to make a small plot to hold small white
crosses dug-in and loosely regimented
with an emblematic poppy of Flanders
black-crimson pinned at the centre of each.
Each hour the cordoned ground expands
to receive more and more bereavements
of every nation that has, with bowed head,
soft-footedly approached on this November day.

A Bay View on Rowntree Park

A windless dawn. Wood pigeons coo,
a walker slides through the philanthropist's
garden — his reflection's dim where an ice
film fails to uphold preening mallards.
A grey squirrel takes in bare branches
leaping from dangled teenage limbs —
sycamore to flowering cherry to oak.
What could've propelled the dawn's
passing screen of eastward mist?

The sun, behind its cold look,
with no ruby fingers extended,
now engulfs my jaded writing desk.
Soon the glow will shave the frost
from child-dedicated lawns and trails.
Already the deep yellow crocus wrestle
from my window-box. To the north
along a shingled dovecote's gable
familiar white wings stay perched.
What could've propelled the dawn's
passing screen of eastward mist?

I remove specs to rub away night,
watch branches reform to mesh.
At my slumped side, tight-lips
of star-gazers bend to the light;
their opening days in the future.
A robin's lilt pierces the closed bay.
And my tired legs absorb the chill
that penetrates this Victorian house...
And what could've propelled dawn's
passing screen of eastward mist?

Oshere or the Unnamed

The night street curves like an unfading gallery.
Behind glass, objects-for-sale turn into artefacts.
Road signs become abstruse as childhood art.

In the city's virtual nullity
who does a No-Entry instruct?
What does a Stop inform?

Out of shop-fronts, like caricatures, displays stare.
What's in season? Relevance alters. Each fractured
hope, or torn faith, shuffles the lines of civilisation.
Again a new portrait appears, a new fad to worship.

At a postern, three large coagula of blood
as if big rubies obstruct the homeward path.
Can no one report the act or its circumstance?
Someone knocks on doors. It's late. Incidents
are too multi-faced for a passer-by to intrude.
A formal, black-suited stranger loiters, then walks
half-away, before hesitating, at a distance, glares back.

Are you at your stall tomorrow, in the delayed dawn air
with propped up fruit and veg, your colourful merchandise
from ungainly boxes that you delight to mangle and fling in
heaps of cardboard and haggled leaves; act more irascible
if you fail to get your way, while the aloof street sleeps?

Upstairs behind a green door, anguish-data's stacked.
Terror grew in households, when a servant's trained eyes
exposed what they shouldn't and flustered hands
misplaced the keys. Along a museum corridor
a twelve-year-old chambermaid's leg-irons dangle
chiselled in stones   the names of *transports*.

A hireling carries his rage into alien rooms and puzzles
from this starving-ground, how can forgiveness grow
that makes bearable the handing-down of days?

Margaret Clitherow sleeps, culted on the eternal aisle.
Her shrine's covey tells nothing of the cloth oddments
she gleaned to sew a death-shirt, to wrap her nakedness.
She faced her accusers un-moved as the abandoned street.
Why step into her martyr's shrine? What do you hope
to detect, sightseers on benches as if in an antechamber
children unwrapping sweets as they scan a curly script?
After slipping coins in a brass slot, what urges you
to turn so abruptly from that unadorned space?
Above scrolled architraves, ordinary rooms contain
taciturn spells. Buildings protrude or stand recessed.
Each facade's mannerism reveals a concealed view
of the thronging passage all merge into. The street has
more secrets to shelter — its closeted prince and princess.

A boy and girl — entwined on a wall — have progressed
as far as they can with emotions they know, the next
step feels boundless. In that leap from modesty they
imagine themselves love-transformed; waking
for each other, in morning's selfless bed, dishabille.

A summer cabby, from his tall seat, gesticulates with
showman's pause, *Famous Shambles — over there!*
from his clip-trotting, carousel-painted, open hackney,
guides visitors through the city's intersecting narrows.

He reins-in the last time and stables his horse. Methodical
cleaners, with over-large brooms, begin to sweep up detritus.
Stalls stretch abandoned. Vacant boards extend like stages —
with poles rising, bound in space — lashed, bolted or nailed —
from many scaffold-focused courtyards. The dark wavers
along terracotta roofs. Creeps by warped steps once cleansed
with carbolic soap. For some, too prompt, daylight's revived.

At the foot of an uncurtained window, in orange glow
three blood-jewels inform, pass on a primal trilogy.
From paving-stone broken glass shouts: *Don't kick us!*
It's bad enough we're broken, though they glimmer
like vestiges, remote as untitled stars. In his lit annex
a conservator re-joins a wounded goblet, a shattered galaxy.

Is it perverse, at the metropolis's heart, night should
settle in, absorb the kinked, funnelled through-passage
while perimeters flare with revelry and recklessness?

Is what survives on the velvet shelf, illusory tomorrow?

A china shop has a paper-face, *Everything Must Go*: Border
Collies, Toby jug, child tea service, willow-pattern vase.
Where's your conscience? Last week you sculled past
refusing to enter, now rush in snatching up bargains.

Along a gallery overrun with visitors, in a monitored
glass case, an over-worked dust-pan and brush rest
beside plainly figured, lavishly creased, pinafores.
Is it unthinkable, they outlast servitude become
integral as art? Absurd that a superfine helmet past
reminiscence, far out of sequence with time, now stuck
with clay and mud, can be recovered from a site's rubble?

Two adolescents relax atop a stone wall on smooth stubs
of sawn-through wrought-iron that mark another era's crisis.
Captured in a conciliatory frame, whole as a sculpted kiss
they may disentangle, yet remain joined. Now,
no longer attainable, they can know
those passions they once yearned.

The night so unattainably loves! Day's understanding
surrenders. With twilight pains, a new generation is culled.

Through sub-hours, before pedestrians start milling, pushing
along winding straits by Cross Keys and Prince's Feathers —
prior to a furtive chorus — a *primum mobile* continues
to link each abandoned right-of-way to undulant space.
So close an estranged presence binds all to unending night.

To that dark absence, is our one response grief, that life's day
can't always evolve, strikes a parasystole, its curfew? What's
the settlement of guileless lovers with that *never-ending*
but their confluence is elsewhere, in un-sequelled night?
Is this the sublime decree to which they, heart-torn, submit?

Past the twelfth din, a stranger's disfigured face speaks
through an iron gate. Discovering the shelter is full
before beginning demented wanderings, he mentions
the scream in the night, to the warden, peering through
the bars, who offers him nothing. Still he persists
with his narrative and lastly claims *It came from*
those opposite but when I looked the windows were blank.

In a cell, under another century's prolonged shadow,
a housewife manipulates needle and thread, sewing
uncountable waste-cuts. Then, led out, she pardons
the masses, as her body is laid flat; her skinny face
against the stone-mounted door. Calmly dismissing,
she succumbs below perhaps blessed stone and wood.

Early, two domestics settle down for a tea break
above the deserted lane. *My husband lived here,*
when these rooms were homes, not businesses. She taps
ash into her red cupped serviette; the other looking on.

A cabby grooms his horse, throwing on a serge blanket,
a market trader claps his hands, stomping broken flags in
a weather-gleam, they know night's legacy, event on event

like an undergarment's compact folds; know its legends,
how round an altar tiers of privileged graves descend.

In a midnight office, a secretary lifts her head from tangled
papers, waiving the old promise — *the next day will bring
a completion* — for an instant gazes, freed from the night.
                    At his dawn hour, an outcast
walks through a cursed green door, up steps to thresholds,
through solitude in rarefied rooms. In a super-inhabited lull,
when humming machines are still, and objects, dispersed
by yesterday's escapees, betray no order for future attention,
for him who endured disgrace, a hushed purgatory goes on.

A long distance driver, an exhausted grip wrenching
round the wheel, steers into a back lane. *This way's
not made for lorries or cars*, says the passenger
piloting him through the inextricable centre.

You, enfeebled, report what you've told over decades
that until you saw his name, listed with the bravely fallen,
in a local post office window, you didn't know that
you loved him and from then on were inconsolable.

On view, at a taxi switchboard, a young woman in
a cerise blouse calls into the black mouthpiece, then leans
back in her swivel chair awaiting acknowledgement.

Who is unaware, why a hermit, in his hand's last stiffening
smothers his relief bell, or what the psalm intimates, written
again and again: *The humble-spirited will possess the earth?*

I have been love-constrained, crouched, dew-soaked,
in a field when the old crescent an outcast to the sun.
Have stooped enthralled at the emptiness in a static-free
message unable to respond with language or mute entreaty.

With a caring physician, stood at the bed of an ancient man
and observed a gullied face, heard a death rattle; prayed for
further breaths; waiting, listening; was allowed one more.

Where stone says: *Thou hast, of thy goodness, prepared*
for the poor where burning initials *Rogue Thief* branded
the guiltless, some hour, out of silent deposits underlying
every epoch the street yields history, transformed. Hands
back a symbol lifted from wreckage, like a Celtic designed
helmet with a Christian inscription. *Oshere* is suffixed
in battered uncials: a name no longer mimicking
a warrior-king, repeating an artisan's pseudonym
or standing as the sign of empire.
                    Oshere is now an appellation
for the present hour's gong, for one under Minerva
handing out leaflets, for some shouting *it's a cock-eyed place,*
others insisting *it's a pother!* for some speechless while others
dedicate a plaque, beyond memory, for a few standing
vigil for peace; fewer, wearing the grey, kneeling.

Last night, we played the Six Bells at darts.
For the first time they were beaten.
Afterwards they were livid, raving...

Later, I slept on the floor
to let a black suited gentleman curl up on my bed...

When shaking on my feet, riding a garrison-town bus
as it nears my stop, I'll need to ask for help.

By King's Square I've skirted an invisible 14th c. church.
And once, in pre-dawn light, I saw the dead assembled
above trampled stones when thinnest white rested on
the branch, saw thinner shapes standing by their graves
sunk in prayer, while I walked past lead monogrammed

guttering with grey rose-badges, from eaves to pavement,
until round the quoin came to an alarm-guarded door.

That dark morning I hesitated before breaking the bond.
Heard, among those lately named by the celebrant
among a series of vanished congregations
the future in sounds of night-watching steps.

Notes

'*Oshere*': is 'an Anglo-Saxon personal name that appears on The York Helmet after the prayer, in Latin, translated 'In the name of our Lord Jesus the Holy Spirit God the Father.' The helmet was discovered in mud and clay a digger had dredged up during excavations for constructing the Coppergate Centre, York. This masterpiece in metal work dates from 750-775 AD. Quote from: The Coppergate Helmet Dominic Tweddle, pub. by Cultural Resource Management Ltd., Jorvik Centre, Coppergate, York, YO11NT, 1984. When I worked as a storage and display care assistant I saw the helmet close up. It is said, the spaces between rivets are so equal that only a computerised measure can achieve such precision now.

'*a twelve-year-old chambermaid's...*': She was convicted of poisoning her master and mistress, perhaps after being sexually abused. Her 'leg-irons' are displayed in the Castle Museum, York.

'*transports*': are supposed criminals who were sent ' to Australia rather than imprisoned or executed. Chiselled names date from the 18th and 19th centuries and can found in pavement stones at the back of the now Castle Museum, previously remains of York Prison, before they were transported.

Margaret Clitherow (1556-86): is a Roman Catholic martyr who lived with her husband (a butcher by trade) with their children along The Shambles. There is now a shrine dedicated to her on the same street.

'*14th Century invisible church*': King Square was the site of Holy Trinity Church, probably the original chapel of the Royal Palace. It fell into disrepair in the late 19th century and was used as sheep pen before demolished in 1937. Now King Square is a central site for street entertainers. The various non-spiritual uses of the Square make it all the more intriguing that I should have experienced a mystical vision there.

'*Among those lately named...*': In some services the names of those who have recently died are read out.'

Summer at No. 8

New owners
restyled the garden,
put in flags and café tables,
severed wild ivy that once
strangled shade offerings of tall beech.
Now overhead each green napkin
freely sings,

from an open pot,
yellow with mocha brown highlights
faces of pansies
are exposed —
the same as my ex-wife's
blousy delicate touch,

between pendant fuchsia
and bleeding hearts
a discursive
hover-fly,

no piped muse,
at a half-open window
a wind-charmer,

a coffee please,
a cappuccino, espresso
he goes up the range,
I say filter
I'm not a regular here,
I feel a cat
approaching
from the blind side —

the owner and her son chat,
dropping the subject, picking it up,

the smell of bread baking settles over me,
they're flexing
for the onslaught of lunch
then their voices turn down
remembering they've a patron
within ear-shot
on the way out
the door squeaks too loud.

Summer Coigns

I

Afternoon Dales Breeds —
perhaps fleeces tangled
by the south easter —
meander overhead
across Iklely Moor's aquamarine.

II

Summer enough
to linger in the botanic garden
a jasmine's night breath —
as if I'm a skeleton —
passing through.

III

Climbing to Raynard Hall
between beryl poplars —
sometimes I've turned to view
a before-glow like this —
one explosion of light

IV

Not seen (as if a youngster
clapped hands over lips
hooted through a grass bowstring
with all the force he owned)
an owl from the sycamore.

V

Beyond an abutment
over burning ridge tiles —
as though Icarus
had achieved his dream —
cloudless, dropping sun.

VI
Along the North Sea corniche
the scent of stunted
hawthorn rolls, while below
with waltzing rhythms
emerald waves come ashore.

VII
Across St Laurence Ginnel —
again I inhale: the same gang
of salmon-pink flowers
obstructing the way.

VIII
Croglin Gorge — footfalls
down the slippery rutted
path — where a fugitive
sought a hiding-place —
by truth-telling water.

IX
After a long day journeying
a few hours in Eagle Wood:
so still, overhead, tiny gaps
in the ancient forest canopy
create new constellations.

I'm Pleased We Have That Window To Look At

To L.M

Tracery facets
through winter brushwork blueing —
a butterfly's wings?

New sheep-skin slippers!
As strolling on clouds: you quip
you'll soon wear them down.

White-particle board…
you press, pat and pattern
a cosmos of sweets.

Sometimes you withhold
letting matter marinate
a week or three months.

Worn dark-grey-shabby
not a hint of whiteness left
my mundane slippers.

Knowing the window's
transcendence, I consider what
lesser sign would do.

I buy you slippers.
Yours, the same style, outlast mine
keep their egg-wash glow.

B.J.'s Tale

Four am, cabbies
round a snack van, stand joshing —
till B.J. hears an owl.

Never heard it, here....
before, the veteran calls out
answering each whooo.

One day, my young wife
vanished. Didn't let her return.
Couldn't take that again.

House-Arrest

For M.W.

I bring her flowers
as I knock on the window
she wakes, smiling, from her chair.

Her eyes ooze confinement.
I praise the tea & sweetmeats
she serves by the fire,

trusting me enough
to retell her fate: a frail dad,
one child-less kind love.

Never deceive me.
She calls me her gentleman
please she staunchly adds.

As I leave she mourns
kisses my lips near the door
Come just when you want

weighing each farewell
with an apple or red rose
she fills my free hand.

Every time she doubts —
I think my talk annoys you —
on her step, waving,

I fear her silence
the great chair she won't rise from
look back, reassuring.

Scotland
and the Isles

At Europe's Edge

black cormorants cling
along igneous skerries

from mica-flaked precipice
we listen to rock's timbre

anthropomorphic
outcrops, earth's *enchaînement*

above volcanic strata
we stroll across a rock bridge

among pinnacles
a bardling's small white flower

grass of Parnassus:
Ben Loyal in view

picturesque and sublime,
landscape genders mell,

below cliff scabious waves roar
in and out of the Cave of the Wind;

unpillared Atlantic, from a scaur
wakes of westward ships

we could perch down there
with wing-furled auks — the shingled globe

singing around us,
along our sight-line

anthropic isles would
interrupt each horizon's fade.

The Rock of Fair Isle

I grovelled with a miser's fingers
under profiles of tide-withdrawn kolls,
raked sandy bullies seeking a holed stone.

Sometimes listening by Ebb rock
eked out to wait inside windowed Kro Stack —
surrounded by hushed turquoise,

other times, winds slamming the compass,
circled by sky-rubbing storms, sighted
marshalling clouds a thousand miles off.

Holms stood like statues round a temple,
one, near-shore, poised, an indolent lion —
its curled head top once an island ness;

with a huff I wedged a small boulder
at daysit, from a salty pool
a shell's ringed concave glistened.

I could imagine everything at mirknin' —
a holed stone for my estranged love,
the moon through a gashed cloud's eye.

High peaked ridges swamped
in spray; where a fore stem was shattered
unharnessed waves rolled over Da Keels.

On the jade North Sea edge
in the ocean's theatre Da Burrian
rose up. When fishing failed

islanders swam to its purple pink cliffs
and brought home in teeth-clenched sacks
swabbie and bonxie's eggs.

Some nights, a patterned scarf round my neck
I walked under the Northern Dancers' embrace —
knitted by an aged crofter's lightning wires.

She rarely told but knew many fates,
after a shipwreck had seen moony shapes
drift over the Bicht ...wavering

like paper dolls. I breathed black shadows
from rivvicks while bereaved voices
echoed through the sunny, oobin day.

Wandered high kames searching...
last night nine fishermen drowned in the Atlantic
now stretching flat as a closed tomb;

below, the week trimmed with bright pools —
reminders of the storm ten that had smashed
the hopes of a necklace-breasted girl.

I saw the Beltane crops turn grey
from a sou'wester and talked with crofters
who'd stepped out fearing their roofs might fly;

on their skelf inside, strangest china
reclaimed from worm-drilled driftwood,
glittered of an age that no-one had yet seen.

I forgot the holed stone and my grief. Breakers
grinded, a yoal was out among snapping whips;
the ocean exploded on the rock of Fair Isle.

Dialect words

bullies = pebbles
kolls = rock faces
eke out = half crawl and walk
holms = tall grass-topped rocks
daysit = end of day
mirknin' = after sun set
fore stem = part of a boat
swabbie = black back gull
bonxie = great skua
wires = knitting needles
rivvicks = narrow gaps in the rocks
oobin' day = peaceful day (after a storm)
kames = grassy slopes where sheep graze
bicht = bay
week = sandy shoreline
skelf = a kind of cabinet shelf
yoal = small fishing boat

Walking the Northern Rim

after reading the Orkneyinga Saga

In an ochre arc —
no boot-prints but our three's
along Torrisdale Bay

> sibilant deer-grass
> foreshadow
> crimson and kindled gold

in Smoo Cave
we're mesmerized
by the voice of origins

> into summer's late sun
> ranked cumulus
> and granite cliffs lean

> we search the Farr Stone
> below chiselled knot-work
> twin birds, necks intertwined

sneaking over mounds
of near-razed Achanlocky —
grieving's provenance

> how many numinous dead?
> we leave unperturbed
> heaped rocks of a cairn

a black beetle rolls
on its four-inch plateau
a ball of sheep's dung

                              vast islanded turquoise
                                 from a high broch
                                a violet hazed scree

at sweet gloaming
over vitreous Loch nan Camh
phragmites hum

                         nibbled by midges
                    who can watch the stars inching
                         from the afterglow?

three lounging grey seals
at the estuary's mouth —
the tide hisses in

                                      over dark Skerray
                                   coils of rain-cloud —
                                    shone constellations

elegantly figured
through a dripping veil
Weaver of the Night

                          intermittently
                    the Maiden sparkles, waiting
                         the Sea's eruption

haunters in the gloom
each silhouetted croft
in oval moonlight

                                   noon water-lilies
                                waver across a lochan
                                Ben Loyal out of mist

baked baps and cheese
at lunch the timbres
of earth's subtle binding

                       from a precipice
              where a saint hugged the coastline
                     Ocean's grey-lapis

above ruckled crags,
against cobalt blue
the pale moon luffs

                          tiny stinging darts
                   guard sea-ploughers' graves
                        from the inquiring

            wrecks of houses —
         over the serpent-sleeping strait
            pattern Eilean Nan Ròn

west wind's home
and guillemots', round igneous
whitened waves' spray

                          almost too alive
                to walk on, this brae, its path
                    so smoothly ascends

over stone-strata
we pause like look-outs: below —
rolling crests battle

              meandering
        water ebbs through a salt-marsh,
           a flock grazing

a wasteland pasture,
who can imagine
its ultimate form?

climbing up higher
and dog-tired above
the surf's smack and punch

sombre narrow rock-gaps
at Port Vasgo echo
the drowned

by a wrecked drifter
mimulus takes root
beyond tidelines

at Talmine harbour
hired-hands hurl back weakling crabs
boxing up the strong

in friendship
a geologist, botanist and me,
brushing through heather

juniper berries
speckled round our aching feet —
where *wolves dined on the dead*

picturesque-sublime
melling *arrow-storm* and peace
along the littoral

scarlet admirals
swift damsel and dragonflies
join in Wee Free dance

> *God Bless* at Lammigo
> the Sea roars in and out
> of the Cave of the Wind

we're highland *gillies*
on vapour-ringed Ben Hope
three white horses nudge

> glacial mirrors
> throw back an unending
> saga of loches

Guide to Langholm etc

for Hugh MacDiarmid

1
His fame cleared disputes.
Beside a triple span bridge
a plaque informs that this
sober, post-industrial
town, was the poet,
the Renaissance man, Hugh
MacDiarmid's first home.
Cannie easily misread rhythms
three river tongues meet.

2
In earthen brown another
signing points to a lane
winding up a brae with
hair-pins to his memorial's
cone of stones that hikers
might mistake as way-markers.
Three decades' moss covering
appears three hundred years
around an embossed poem
to home in Scot's dialect.

3
MacDiarmid's words set.
Higher up the vantage,
an overstated spire
that the wealthier town
erected a century before
shows off another man's
labour and philanthropy.

No honour in a speaker's gift
that doesn't stir conviction
the poet, the nation shaker,
the recluse, might've argued
raking his hands through his hair
that shot upright in a blast
from his runkled forehead
when he relaxed, nursed a pipe,
with literary comrades.

4
Beyond textiles' clatter
and gentlemen's looting,
after all the controversy
and despotic delusions
(some riverbank urchin
could have seen through)
the carved wood thistle
knocker, on his blue door,
gives a tempered welcome
to the next writerly pioneer.

5
Outside his last cottage's
early March muskiness,
the wind reforms landscape
to cloud. Summits in steps, rise,
each higher and more wasted.
In between in Lanark haze,
glens, pitted with crannies,
avoid the viewer's gazing
where he explored before
his next visible ascending.

Hugh MacDiarmid

With all his global hype
it's two valleys westward
to the poet's last home.
Brownsbank views hold
kind remembrance of this
modern, dedicated man
each hill's fall and glide
whatever rant or politics.
Perhaps he forgot hatreds
as snow turned to cherry
blossoms in wall-guarded
garden, or the fire's ember
or a loving hand reposing
on his wrist comforted him
beyond his old extremes
to that point of praise
from where it all began.

Ben Nicholson
Miniatures

In the Gallery

Nothing but a chair.
I long to leap the rope-barrier
settle next to his genius.

Fallen white corners
the exhibition: exquisite designs
spaced along walls.

On differing planes
lucid forms rise and recede
setting lineaments.

His paintings ask the viewer
to be roused by nothing
by absent emotions.

Child-soft, age-timid,
jumbled in elementary order:
one quiet masterpiece.

Viewing infinity
through the gallery window
lead facets vanish.

Between worldly fears
compassion might prevail
seeking highest abstract.

The Works of Art

Untitled (1945)
Without words to ask,
hear a communication
of angles and circles.

Still Life (1945)
A lull
so vivid, colour perturbs
empty space.

Lirkion (1963)
Through prominent lines
further connections imply
hidden time rehearsed.

Four (1958)
Partly square islands consent,
but how? through space, when?
two with bold divides.

Arbia 2 (1957)
Overlaying form,
patterns; not one complete
until everything's whole.

Argolis (1959)
Bordered by brown, some rise:
others through thin blueness float,
pictures in pictures.

Travertine (1961)
Before language-sense
language-nonsense speaks
to an all-involving heart.

Urbino (1965)
Currents, slender and thick,
lead to darkness, to grey-wash,
then russet intrudes.

Circle and Venetian Red (1966)
Beauty's hard, complete,
uncompromising, runic-scratched
its meaning long lost.

Sunion (1960)
Even the sun's child
might've dropped his reckless scheme
for this unending circle.

Relief (1960)
Not as though allies,
yet in dialogue, still slightly opposed,
between them rounded peace.

Still Life (1961)
Landscape with vessel
unfinished, beyond greyness
glows obscurity.

Interlocking   (1962)
Their outlines
persist, one absence
overlacing the other.

Pathos: Project for Free-Standing Wall   (1964)
A harmless builder
may've begun; gave up to just play
on these vast stones.

Altamira 2   (1966)
Gothic arch and chalice
cross at one point, half-formed,
suspended in space.

Bottle, Plate, Goblets   (1959)
Before dispersed
into fragments: shapes gripped
in the act of separation.

Pistoia   (1956)
Through an impenetrable wall
naiveté forges an eye
to an inner mood.

Stone Relief, Valle Verzasca   (1964)
Cosmic stairs are awkward
with no landing —
toward the highest abstract.

West Cornwall (1955)
As isles, around images
black curls here and there margin
faint though clear motifs.

Karia (1965)
Limbs disjointed,
without pain, bound to threads
circuiting beyond.

Paros (1959)
Smaller and greater
circles intersect, creating
a complex frontier.

Olympia, Project For Free-Standing Wall (1960)
Vistas unified
supported by locking-join
colour's gradation.

White Columns (1956)
Clear lines partly shaped,
objects piled on objects
cause levitation.

Saronikos (1966)
A red plane floats on grey
then grey widths float on blue then —
colour has no door.

Still Life (c.1950)
A way of seeing turns
into infinity's dimension:
one tea cup, one jug.

Galileo (1963)
Three universes,
black maps, adrift and attached,
two with level spheres.

Worlds in trio
almost collide, but stay passive
moving on two endless squares.

What denotes form
that's formless, that gradually
toward death brightens?

Circles in Granite (1961)
Dust-refined fields
half-coincide, never conflict:
one immense stone stage.

Arezzo 2 (1956/59)
How can disarray
of indefinite shapes slip into
marble's restfulness?

Lindos (1959)
A glass door, perhaps,
a window, but there's nothing beyond
this perfect threshold.

Shell   (1960)
Structureless structure:
what is it you can lift up
see through, hear from?

Travertine   (1961)
Who can make out this design —
linking sponge-textured mix-colour blocks?
In the background, less clues.

Urbino 2   (1965)
In an earthen-figure
a stoic contrast
turns to thinness, black, greyness.

Mycenae 3, Brown and Blue   (1959)
From many profiles
exudes — sacred and untelling —
lunar peacefulness.

A short night's quest
enters a possible labyrinth
as a way to totality.

Circle and Ventian Red
(Project For Free-Standing Wall)   (1966)
Soft scribbles on stone,
the work's half-done
that gleams as finished.

Monte Alcino   (1955)
Depth and shallowness play.
Bottles, wineglasses criss-cross
on tables on countless plateaus.

Coral   (1958)
What phase
can this be: the moon's round
and not yet full?

Still Life   (c.1961)
Interior landscape:
some indistinct well of light
far beyond a transparent jug.

Off-White Relief. Paros   (1959)
Abstracted from the whole:
but what's the final backdrop
for endless stages?

Still Life   (1958)
Not drifting. Hollow shapes —
inscribed by the viewer's breath —
blown ashore.

Granite   (1956)
Trampled? Never once stepped on?
Tireless erosion has scarred
these nonrecurring rocks.

Persian Lilac   (1953)
Form bends toward formless
colour toward colourless,
light-grey-black blossoms.

Tregeseal   (1956)
No equals survive:
odd circles, angle cut moulds:
symmetry cannot be lost.

What gives form presence?
Textured rocks painted on wood
create seried perspectives.

Great circle, the sun,
lesser, the moon, each shadows
earth's square mystical plane.

Still Life   (c.1962)
The mapless charted:
contours infer jug, plate and table,
enclose an untracable void.

2 Goblets — Piero   (1958)
Black and white,
a pair wedded, continue
unformed, detached.

White Relief. Paros   (1962)
Serenely over-laid —
like a tower —
grow from their extremes.

Stone Facets   (1956)
A network
of grey configurations
veils more sketchy intents.

Campanile. White Relief   (1955)
No depth or height,
mind conceives flawless ground
an open dot.

The eye
discovered
peering into an off-camera scene.

Fiesole   (1963)
Dissonance —
blue, black, grey-blue, green-gold, red —
inter-plays.

Colour vacancies
over-lapping, never
imply an end.

Rockscape   (1963)
Prolonged watching
of four fixed, levelled mountains,
regrets seem dust.

Kos   (1959)
From an underworld
arise, transformed
into guileless voyeurs.

Arezzo 1   (1956)
Hall of mirrors:
images upright at first,
then, clatter.

Game of pick-up sticks:
who has the skill to lift,
discriminate, disentangle?

Flower of a Lime Tree   (1956)
No tree, no Spring,
no witnessing greens or streets;
unconfinable space cradled.

Lipari   (1957)
Cohering, nothing's stuck,
varied angles hold; unanchored,
perspectives look in, look out.

Bull Frog   (1962)
A fathomless depth
formed by a line's long sweep —
before conception.

Painting   (1937)
One way's pitch black.
There's always red's smaller rectangle
at grey's other door.

In absolute calm
colours and shapes — not one the same —
create each other.

Tea-Pot, Mugs, Cups and Saucers   (1930)
Patterns simplified,
seeing remotely or through
the tablecloth fades.

White Relief. Paros   (1961-62)
Brave, concertined,
pillars inside of pillars rise up —
at any point — fall.

Argina 2 . Off White Relief.   (1965)
As if more than a key:
two forms, dark and light-grey, locked,
none to ask the code.

Stone's kindest vastness,
no one hurts and none to forgive,
distance achieved.

Not lifeless:
— notched, filed, smoothed,
polished — might open death.

Menhir   (1956)
A shock, the break seems.
After long looking down the route
appears predestined.

Silver Brown   (1957)
Silver, brown, tin, rust:
can colour supplant form,
form colour?

Still Life Birdie (1934)
No one with wisdom
to capture red, or black,
never mind what's between.

An idea eludes, returns,
escapes, before vanishing into
black or red contentment.

Copernicus (1962)
The universe so calm,
no terror. At one point
four horizons meet.

Poised
a small to a greater,
two aligned circles.

Measured precisely
by a telescopic eye
four infinites merge.

Night Facade (1955)
What more deeply hems-in
this complex plane that light centres?
Black nearly green remains black.

Briefly day inscribes
moulded blues, reds: yellow-focused
with one window.

Stronger than chance
thin lines proceed, straight or curved; some,
bold white through darkness.

Poisonous Yellow (1949)
Things slip from relevance:
wholeness enfolding the finite
till nowhere a handle.

Alnwick (1961)
What nonexistence
beyond linked bottle,
vase, circle, goblet and glass?

Greystone (1966)
Between form's integrity
and surface quietude
a thought mediates.

Stonehead (1964)
Glacial artefact:
red's so smooth, lines carved so square,
a human enterprise?

Seven Pillars of Wisdom (1943)
Absence connects
thin, dark cuts and circles:
becomes foundation.

Things that took centuries
to construct — described
in an empty moment.

No one knows the meaning
long mislaid or too far ahead.
Some attempt observance.

Painted Relief. Version 1   (1939)
Massive beginnings
closeby subtle conclusions:
not sure what intervenes.

Painted Relief   (1935)
Each, from a square —
one lens gapping, the other shut —
illuminates unknown.

Composition   (1939)
Too accurate
for child genius: too simple
for finesse.

Who builds innocence?
Sea-blue and coal's flattened black,
a small scarlet bridge.

Blue fills the right,
nothing's fierce. Nothing timid
black occupies left. Red conceals the heart.

Mousehole   (1958)
Leaving the harbour:
somehow the most fragile boats set sail
for the highest abstract.

Contrapuntal   (1953)
Never completed
one mystic jig-saw puzzle,
not a piece missing

Delos   (1954)
All form emerges
from the formless. Tense in the act
lines start to connect.

In goblets, amphoras
origins remain, enclosed
through shape's clarity.

Each re-mould recalls
immense emptinesses. Can fates
be styled or designed?

Faint or bold, lines or colours
expose nothing
except what's beyond form.

Can we arrive there
and not be dead? Who knows?
Somehow, sometimes it happens.

Two Forms   (1940-43)
Pondering twins,
contrasts and congruities
produce a third.

Still nothing alters
the slim 'never-ending' between
for the eye to conceive.

A dual, in silence,
so immobile, time and space
bleed into colourless.

Unseen: curvy nudes,
passionate, revealed as love's
sleeping abstracts.

Pressed so near,
elevated, both
still hold back desire.

Two forms — one in light
opened, one in dark closed —
entrances to the infinite.

Moonrise   (1974)
Continuous curve
almost gone in the infinity
of a lop-sided square

Night blue and brown circle   (1975)
Nothing left to turn...
mistaken door after door
to an unwindowed space

Invisible circle   (1970)
It can be imagined:
passion of a symmetry
that lightly touches

Obidos, Portugal 1   (1971)
No margin for sky —
at peace a flag's burning mist
blown out to extreme

Obidos, Portugal 3   (1971)
Always a loss to see
the ghost in the mirror — not
its becoming or fade

Obidos, Portugal 2   (1971)
No killer could make
lines so nightmarishly warped —
a half-washed off stain

Dolphin   (1971)
thing within a thing
aglow: nearly occupying
still incomplete

Silverpoint   (1971)
bolt of blindness,
the rest: layers of light
in levitation

spanners Holkham 3   (1973)
Such a heart leak
only weightless spanners
& pliers can repair

spanners in movement   (1973)
Before life's door
I dream the tools needed
to construct my ship

scissors variations on a theme no 4   (1968)
Twin facing scissors
like Pisces or Ying & Yang
can't cut a way out

My house I figure
on the slant, now the night sky's
taken up lodging

I reject no object.
Anything could turn into art
in mad moments

It sounds loony
a crescent's a crescent
whether steel- or shadow-made

spanners and holes 4   (1973)
An old workman came...
tools left began to float
like overlapping lily-pads.

ivory   (1979)
Some lines turn into routes —
curving so narrow — that can't
go on except with wings

interior cathedral   (1981)
One form partly erased
another's outline intact
half-absent behind a third

untitled — brown and black   (1981)
A red walk into
a deep maze — that someone's
just started to build

mountain side   (1981)
Light glissading down
through pale blue or orange wash makes
the hills transparent

Castagnola   (1981)
Who set this last table?
misshapen bowls, jugs and cups
sublimely arranged

several forms   (1981)
Some things keep their shape
yet are invisible — to show
love's highest terrain.

Erymanthos   (1966)
steps down if they're stone
are deep stained: on one edge red
the other turquoise

symbol underfoot:
a circle, crossing a line, fades,
frontier, vanishes.

Carnac, red and brown   (1966)
it seems a barrier
too beautiful to want
to avoid or overcome.

Greek Island   (1965)
surface: thin painted
squares, rectangles allow veins
of grief to creep through

Capraia   (1965)
such passionate space
denying the body's touch
longs to be cuddled

ice — off — blue   (1960)
if ends and beginnings
could be disentangled — we'd only
yearn to arrange them as before

always delusion
to sense no desire, look, a halo
round some right angles

in places sheets
whitish blue darken, look to thaw
without losing their edge.

Cyclades   (1959)
in endless washed out surf
one so dark red island —
a voice at last heard

but its bluey foreshore
as if silence and speech first
met some age ago

white relief — Paros   (1962)
upright rectangles shade
into the absolute — leaving
thin shadows behind

Agros   (1960)
Too shy to arrive?
here at every corner —
a stepping off the plane.

blue rock   (1961)
you need search for it,
if it's a colour, among
browns, yellows, whites

Olympic fragment   (1963)
who falls into this tall
non-mirror, wishes nothing
happens but what does

blue rock   (1961)
could be the last door
to open: gazing on it
there's no need to enter

Olympic fragment   (1963)
behind carved dark wood
light persists, which first was in front
sketching the dream.

Capraia   (1965)
passionate absence
denying the body's touch
longs to be embraced

no-one can believe
a passionate absence
blushes in retreat

Lyric Sequence for No One

'We love the earth only through woman,
and the earth in turn loves us.'
ANTON BRETON

'Every place that is not feminine cannot be trusted.'
IBN AL-ARABI

'Woman is the radiance of God; she is not your beloved.
She is the Creator — you could say that she is not created.'
MEVLANA JALALUDDIN RUMI

I

Squirrel in the Park

On that coat-wearing July day the sun in and out
you and I cuddled on a barely dried park bench; you
leaned back into me. And my arms encircled, under
your breasts, tenderly pressing those pleasure curves.

A grey squirrel jumped on to the four gnawed planks
of our seat and squatted beside. You broke a morsel
of rock cake, stretched your hand with dipped fingers.
And it came near, keen eyes, pricked ears, its snout

twitched; fine as a tongue's caress it took the sultana
titbit from your soft skin, out of your palm. And you:
That's never happened before. It sprang to the top

of the seat's back to twirl the chunk in agile claws —
a triumphant juggler. Next, scratched and nosed our
carrier. *It likes sultanas.* Its scent blended with yours.

II

Lincolnshire Hills

Evening thunderclaps grounded a field of magpies.
You and I drove on with sky expanding to new light.
I like this Lincolnshire roll. I took in rain-glistened

heath land. We pub-leapt from Dunston to Scopwick
past puddled concrete to World War II airmen's graves,
across a humped child-like bridge, circling ducks below.

You shimmered in your Klimt smooth dress, a pearl string
teasing its quiet V's plunge. *Shall we get dressed up?*
earlier you'd asked. Now you praised my long satin tie.

Taking more sips, we relaxed in another pub, guessed
its Georgian tastes. Kept touching, stroking, *like a rash.*
Then out, under ivy frontage, into twilight's purple fall.

An owl hooted. On the road again, now north by west.
Evading last clouds, the sun dropped, an orange flare
beyond the outline of old Colby Glen's watch tower.

Each night-closing mile your hand pressed my thigh.
I forgot the warm-cold adage. From that imposing palm
secret warmth spread, locking the future with your seal.

Hardly awake, I only yearned for the light in your eyes,
sped through cliff villages, past Waddington, toward hugs
and kisses in a flash-flood, tanked up with happiness.

III

Pheasant

Our passage tilted, snaked and narrowed. You sat
close, gauging my speed. We climbed, parted low hills
between rounded hedgerows with no demands on time.

You navigated. The map spread across your thighs.
I urged routes to never imagined places. The road's
blacktop dimmed and sometimes vanished beneath

flicking hedge-shadows. For no reason, I slowed.
From the verge a pheasant, its head and eyes raced
on toothpick legs; its feathers a colourful shroud.

I swerved. From the right, it shot into the left's shade.
Your cheeks darkened, your mouth dilated to *OOO*
in fright and relief. What would've killing it meant?

Those days, I wanted to do everything for us: which
signs to follow, best landscape to drive through, when
to stop, to go? Your wrist laid, on the road atlas, thin

as a fledgling's neck. I imagined under denim, the soft
giving groove between your legs. *Hey, how about this turn?*
'Where?' I wondered, in what you coined my sexy voice.

IV

Burrowing

You arrived before time, a coy morning kiss from cool
faintly pale lips. We waited on the near empty platform.
Our minutes joined and passed like coupled carriages —
one foreshadowing the next. I felt your coat's warmth.

You let me travel your arm, wrist to shoulder. My fingers
teased the space under your sleeve and its synthetic fur-cuff
a bit speckled, glistening like a polished violin. You smiled
at me having fun searching out that tender, curved burrow.

Later, climbing to the city's Castle, you strangely shivered
and ached, re-living another distant stairway. That location
shaped our present vista. I longed to share your ascent.

On the train home, after Newark the passengers thinned out.
We traded our pasts, told stories of oceans and harbour islands.
This journey's never been as fast. That too, I took as praise.

V

One Early Evening in a Restaurant

On another day we stumbled on, mis-reading the city.
Then, almost at its cultural quarter's edge, a Balti place.
We shuffled through a bruised door that I held back,
soon a solo waiter swept us to a prime corner seat.

We sat close, joined at the hip, glancing over menus
at vacant tables and high-backed chairs. The waiter,
with all-the-world's time, jotted down our wishes. We
recalled our afternoon, sure that special day was ours.

Poppadums in Mango Chutney. Somehow I frowned.
You saw doubt, turned and set your whole focus on me.
Under lashes, hardly rising, your hazel eyes inquired.
A sweet breath escaping through your made-up lips

pronounced, *Believe me, I'm with you.* We'd both stood
beside another, heard vows spoken, traded gemstone signs.
I echoed your ring-bright phrase. We didn't call the waiter

for red wine, to toast, but clicked water-brimmed goblets:
to be transformed, for simplicity, to set every future free?
Your trembling face, daubed with loss, blushed with hope.

VI

Tingling

That night, you entered in purple. A smocked neckline
stretched away to the peak of each smooth shoulder.
Through eyelets your blouse front was tied with laces

with two dangling ends. Further down an oval opening,
a tear-drop window, as though a baby whale's blow-hole,
gave a glimpse of your seductive cleavage. You collapsed

into heaped up pillows. And I hammocked you in my arms.
Your face soothed against mine, lashes flicked my cheeks.
Your kissing mouth imprinted a long trail from ears to lips
to eyelids, back across my forehead while my hand stroked

your legs, back and forth inside your skirt from your knee's
hollow, to the thigh up to the hip. Your hand grew into a star-
fish, your fingers reached out wide against my shirt's front.
One tip intrigued each button, easing them from their holes.

Drapes left un-pulled, the warm night spilled in, a shining
menagerie. You turned, spoke something into my ear's whirl.

VII

Minster and Flowers

'Where would you like to go?' I asked. *Where'd you?*
'The Minster.' *That sounds nice.* In its Chapter House

we scanned grey leaves, tempted to caress fleshy stone.
Your gaze helped me feel its silent, forbidding curves.

I perhaps helped your looking? You guided my eyes up
to an iconic portrait peering from a boss like a soul mate.

I directed along aisles, across the sun-freckled transepts
until, on a wall, traces of rouge paint revealed a youth's

enthused eyes, grape-flush with love and yet circled with
fear past reverie as if he'd seen everything sacred crushed.

Outside, we stopped and watched young volunteers, on steps,
nursing the east door's wood, daubing it with dark oily cloths.

Lacing our hands, maybe a little alarmed we couldn't sightsee
the future, we crept on to a cream tea under perfumed baskets.

And to yours — *A woman, sometimes, desires to be pampered* —
I placed across your open arms a bouquet of star-gazing lilies.

VIII

Most Pleasurable Day and Night

Head-high sedges nudged. We strayed along a green canal.
I showed how the current gushed, and further on flowed
in the reverse direction. You were patiently impressed.

We walked on into coolness and shade under a bridge.
You stepped gingerly to keep your heels from slipping.
Your pink painted toenails glowed between your shoes'

thin black straps. I wished to hoist you up. Lift you across.
Please, understand, you'd explained, *I'm not able to go far.*
The day had shifted so quickly from urban to country views

it appeared our long afternoon had been snatched from reality.
A boy from a boat's chrome bow at last looked, then waved.
We turned away. And along another track, arrived at a gate

where a white horse lingered, we imagined for us. Its high
head and cloud-fast mane ready to lift us on hidden wings.
Swiftly you unzipped your green fleece, inviting me inside.

Later, you asked: though I'm ill, would you like me to stay?
Embracing, as passion's current rushed on, I didn't dream
in one night how many kisses might flow from your lips.

IX

Illness and Innocence

Another caring, loving, easy day dwindled.
You unlinked your imitation pearls, releasing
with both hands a minute catch on your nape.
Unnoticed, some must've scattered on the floor.

You pulled the bedclothes up high to your chin
and in the same breath asked, *Do you just want
to sleep tonight?* You turned your pale skin away
and concealed the oyster white of your Venus navel.

I looped feebly a spare arm over your back trying
as much as I could to squeeze in close. My belly
riding on your quivering arced spine, I felt your
scent, but not the promise of our hoped-for years.

Illness was a tease, a trick, a glancing grin or
a guest concealed inside until fatal to the whole.

X

Next Morning

You, too deliberately, tied those fluffy flaps of your
dressing gown; closed out my 'longing for you' gaze.
Like a deep seer you turned remote and unhuggable.

Later, your fingers strained to re-join that necklace
the shadow of last night's nimble struggle. And you
made the link unaware that some globes were missing.

After a while, as if recalling something, your flicked
your eyelashes, glanced up at me, grasping my arms,
holding me still, begged my eyes to surrender to yours.

I saw beside your green top's neckline that one of your
flesh-colour bra straps was awry and might be in view.
I attempted to correct it; but then let the flaw continue.

I should've known, did know, but allowed every sign to
steal past, yearning for your return for many pearl-hours.

XI

It seems strange to write another piece, after years have lapsed. Was it illness or another man who carried you away? At the time, the answer was self-evident, now I'm in doubt. I recall an event you mentioned, during our loving days. You were far out in the ocean, past harbour islands, when young, but already married to a mariner, a deep-sea fisher, a good man. You saw a blue Marlin snap the taut unspooled fishing lines and escape, its scaled back gleaming. You rejoiced. You were happy, you said, sailing far and wide, as if out of touch. With what? Yet, other men were soon enough hunting after your beauty. You learned you had power to give pleasure and pain, and to gather in those twins with equal candour. Already you knew your flesh was a terrible lure and treacherous — inflicted with an illness that warned you would never hug your own children. Your husband, naive about your pursuers, was unhelpful about your diseased womb. When the first anchor-hold slipped, you were left with the skill to arouse and suffer from bed-sit to palace, from back street to hidden curved driveway, from hope to hopeless. Your future unreeled. No sex goddess or courtesan, you ached too much at the loss of a soul mate, at each fresh departure or re-entry. I see that blue Marlin, one last time. Perhaps it is you, a sparkling beauty wounded, pulling all the islands of the world to the ocean's rim.

War Associations

The Seasons

This Easter early...
Spring comes early too
to greet the stranger

Tamer than the rest
a toddler stretches and pats
one sheep's hornless head

Among the thorns
a wild donkey stuttering —
still with a cross on its back

At far Mablethorpe
on a shiny August day
children ride the sand

Listen: water-song
beneath island willow's shade
let's never come out

No longer crimson
scarlet or green; windfallen
by a hedge — apples

Stunted grey elder
— how many years in making
its gold lichen sleeves?

Across Coleby Grange
now unable to settle
November snowfall

1969

Two youths, strangers on a campsite,
one Canadian, the other American,
shoot an NFL football back & forth
among shoreline pines of Michigan.
Brown polished spirals shattering
passive green. Ducking, faking we
run patterns pro-style, knife-precise
catching one toss at the boot straps,
even full stretch a juggling one-hander,
until every limb aching we crash down
on a spare picnic table's bench to chat.
'What' y' doin' after summer?' I ask.
— *I'm going to Vietnam. And you?*

Thinking of My Father at Monte Cassino, 1944

As if I was a child who only knew a father by a grave
as though a mother who only knew birth by a sonogram
your hazy words speak to me of the enormities of war.

I have fingered the battle-site on the ordinances of Italy
and scratched the write-ups, noting the counted dead,
have dwelt on your survival and the echoes of victory

that sound more faint with each year's eclipse. It's not
as metaphor or statistic, I can imagine you, but only as flesh
clenching steel, the Ack Ack's jolt when a shell was fired,

your hands drooping when you mourned a comrade soul's
release, but mostly your rising hatred towards the enemy
as if that was the only way back to loved ones and peace.

The Mermaid's Chair

An oceanic perfume clings
to the hand-carved mermaid
who genuflects on sacred scales

as her exposed mid-drift bulges
with its wood navel sublimely
rounded as any far-seeing eye.

She holds a quince and comb
in moonless harmony. Her hair
glistening as she looks ready to

ripple like an oriental dancer
letting her skirt's waist shimmy
low just below the hip line.

Yet, since no one can help
conceive her fated off-spring,
she'll never need to disrobe.

She watches long and knows
beyond sea faith and land faith —
love survives each era's wreckage.

Stories from
the USA

A Road Poem

(Two Brits and an American)

1

We'd each hit middle age from separate roads.
Now, a trio in a white Pontiac, we headed down
bumbling ways, past apple orchards and cornfields;
through our half open windows, the passing land
rolled by with tall verges and with bird-chatter.
A warming breeze penetrating. At least the cool
Spring seemed finished. Approaching the Illinois
we glided through Meredosa, 'an old river town'
your friend called it as if on a less travelled route.
We were charmed by dilapidated looks: a plywood
board chapel, faith stain-glass intact, a porch-roof
precariously angled among tall maples, and further,
'For Sale' signs on lacy pillars time hadn't wrecked.
A scarlet tanager flitted, dived through blue and white
crowd of stars and stripes. Far too early for a ceremony,
prim flags flapped, newly grown there, as if someone
had planted them during last night thunderstorm when
most citizens were asleep. We crossed the barge-lined
Illinois, over a 1930s' suspension bridge, gazing down
at the brown water looking to forecast our destination.

2

The road always quiet. We evaded tourist box turtles
wading in across the tarmac. Re-fuelling by credit
card, kept to the same highway, once or twice alerted
by four-way stops, as invidious as roundabouts. We,
a male and two females, I was the driver; you and her
long-time companions who hadn't seen each other

for ages till now. With four lanes we drove through
outskirts Quincy's Memorial Day moods; between
strip malls and box stores, the gaunt North American
town guardians. Halting for stop lights, it all seemed
like the hard casing to the pliant city. Your friend's
home town; she knew its intimate ways, under her
natural guidance we felt more than tourists. But she
wasn't sure which street went right down to the river.
The past settlement had befriended once homeless
Joseph Smith, his tablets and his Mormon pilgrims.
All that had distantly retreated under encrusted
history: slaughter of indigenous, civil war, depression,
post war world domination, new attacks, US revenge.
You said, as the roadway in front peaked, looked to slide
toward some universal divide, a conclusion of sorts,
'The Mississippi must be ahead. It's like approaching
the sea, that feeling as you near land's end'. I drove on
non-committal with a water smell enthusing thought.

3

You and I British, and your compeer, an American...
recalling this land was once your stomping ground
for a season. I turned my motives, why desire to reach
this continental current — what was yours? And your
old friend who so quickly agreed to our adventure?
So following you, I found myself half way across
the map. Perhaps I intended to recover something
from those depths, from its shifty flux, sandbars
and snags. Travelling might mean to see this republic
as more than some boogie land wrecking the world —
to undo easy European viewpoints. Now trouble-free
the town sloped from bluffs with no sign of mastery.
I'd come to the Mississippi for some renewal that
would shake my Brit Anti-Yankee assumptions.
I was a new-worlder too, born this Atlantic side.

4

Outside, on the river's muddy rim we had sandwiches
as the cloudy sun stung with a brief, hot appearance.
Your friend reminded us, if reports were correct, that
this was the last day we'd be swatting at buffalo gnats.
From a dock, a few boatmen puttered; passing the 'No
Wake' notice, hit the throttle, lunged their prows up!
A giant waterbed before us, each speed boat's roar
diminished north or southward, lost to the enormity.
Unlike chirpy red-wings we deserted our picnic perch
to seek a better look, unimpeded by rail or road spans.
No artistic bridge across, where the swaying expanse
unschooled moved between a nation's shoulder blades:
the brown blood river, unknown, vital. We searched on
by houses on spidery stilts above recorded flood lines,
through fenland terrain, flood plains. Until we sighted
a geese colony in black shadowed bars of old maize
their tall necks among, between half-smashed stalks.
Camouflaged, they hardly moved across your camera's
feral gaze. At the other ditch, I feared a beast could strike
like lightning if I plodded into its merging waterways.

Backwaters, marshy pools re-carved channels, we came
to 'Road Closed' red; the green bank would stay unvisited.
The River: a muddy off-shoot washed over the tarmac.
A yellow-down meadow lark gripped a mud-stuck branch
projecting from the chocolate smoothness. You, out of the car,
prodded at the slimy brink, thinking of wading in to cross.
A mulch sedimentary reek lingered. We (you back beside me)
reversed and turned away. I remembered you had often
pressed to some edge, beyond reason's guide rails, to be
near to a thing great, inconspicuous, dangerous and wild:
Australia in the outback, Cape Cod in winter, and some
where unnamed. On that shore you had to fend off a young
man's love, as if an edge foreshadows retreat every time.

5

We had to give up the master-plan. Instead follow our
host's guidance through straight street mazes of houses.
We reached a 1906 park with black poplars in an avenue.
Along another cliff top a first explorer's inveterate statue.
He gazed out from here towards the end he could forecast.
A gigantic water-snake pulsed between limestone heights.
But he leaned back as if resting against his future fame,
fear and doubt sucked from eyes. He knew he must cross.
We pushed on to see a local man's Moorish castle folly
on a further ridge, above neck-high fences and rail yards.
One car in the parking lot, we wouldn't pay for a tour.
So edged on, right, left, right, trying to find Quincy's
inner groomed quarter with wide tree-hooped streets.
Long front lawns proceeded to wraparound porches
through neighbourhoods with houses nick-named San
Francisco ladies, pink and green, flamingo and parrot,
where out-size driveways hugged their motor-pool
where passing cars sneaked on pillow-tread wheels
under foliated shade, bouquet iris beds at corners
where litter was alien as hardship or ruckus music...
game-board luxury boulevards, blue square properties
along Jersey to Kentucky, off Main, back to 18th St.
We cruised, not for burgers or pick-ups, but crawled
through enclaves of wealth, rest and success (what
freedom can achieve) a repose far from Mississippi
and holiday Malls and yet always brushed by them,
so we sighed too for idylls that are illusionist tricks.
You exclaimed 'it's nature I prefer, when no structures
face me'. I was shocked, after you'd praised so much
high-brow real estate. And yet none of us at ease.

6

Something else more intimate than strangers' pretty
plots, but I couldn't get to it: your friend's pleasure
to be here, taking up our aims, to come to her old home,
not on urban plantations or in German Historic Districts,
but just the same somewhere among warmth and light
a past resided, needed contact, a mother's grave visiting
and yet I couldn't see past my longing to hold the River
here and now. You, my accomplice, we drove South,
down interstate 72, out of the way to another landing:
Hannibal, Missouri, across the divide, looking back.
It seemed wilder on this side, without an explanation,
but we found a stranded log, it must've escaped from
a sawmill, a gigantic specimen, its ends cut straight off,
now stranded on the slimy bank, rolled in by backwash,
resting until the unpredictable river tide flows again
chasing it on for another thousand miles. We looked
back at a far shore, the just passed beach-line, already
a fantasy land. We'd stumbled on Mark Twain's home:
his bold Tom Swayer and raft, his front porch despair.
A freight train slid between town and near shore-bed
its emphatic overture, a horn's preclude blast held us
stock still. Its chorus ricocheted across sloppy brown
waves. They may've heard it in Illinois or maybe not.

7

Your companion remembered a far distant boyfriend,
'He loved dumb trains and used to court me at stations.
Made songs from numbers, names that rickey-tick passed'.
Lovesickness I guessed. Box cars and engines, I thought
of destinations, remembered my high-jinks when I wanted
a woman to walk in 10 feet of snow to prove her affection.
It was about proving, not believing in love. The town was
dressing down; late afternoon in a flag-lined thoroughfare.

Snack vendors were closing up after a fair or celebration.
And everyone was leaving. We just managed ice creams,
knocking on the window of a closed, old style general store.
The wind heated. Thunder rat-a-tatted across now split sky.
We ran for shelter; didn't make it so were soaked through
by the Mississippi as a last seller grinned shutting his trailer.
We shared a roofed look-out with a dog and a boastful child
who harped on that he was mostly dry and we mostly wet.
So, the weather half-clearing, we ventured out, arriving at
a replica Steam Boat moored, planks down for passengers
about an hour before evening sailing, jazz band and dinner.
Mark Twain was everywhere, in the boat's name, in candy
and the off-river homestead. For some reason, we declined
the steamer's hooter and belch; stayed on quivering shore.

8

Pleasure and dejection, we strolled down the main street,
drying off, almost deserted, past his museum glass front.
He was in a photo series, in a white suit in a rocking chair
on a white verandah looking river-wards, veiling despair.
An inner query arose: why wasn't it enough to be known
and be famous; why couldn't best words heal always? But
I countered myself, we have only language, replicas for
the day that actually happened, which passed un-gripped.
I included your phone-snap shots that so-called captured.
You'd wanted to get those fancy turn-of-century benches
in the Park; at least one, you ordered, with no person in it,
no reference. I thought, strange. Our day was passing away
unrecorded as a boy's punting down the quagmire river.

9

At last, from stop-light tangled Hannibal, we spun for
home, for your peer's trusty apple farm, where we'd bed

down for the night. In England, our further home, for years
we'd worried on the macro-scale about eroding eastern cliffs
North Sea's invasive force; ancient coast-towns threatened.
But, here, finding a blunt arrow pointing to the interstate, we
fretted more simply, whether the sky was black, the day hot
enough to create a tornado. Back in the riddling town's heart,
two stars and stripes tourists had said, 'Bad storm...comin',
noting our half-lost demeanour. The heavens and the streets
passively disposed. But from a clambering bar, through glass
that left no walls, males faces leered at us walking strangers,
with a predatory stiffness that didn't care a hoot for anyone.
I'd felt we should escape, whatever that meant, back across
the river. Memorial day, remember the dead, had become
somehow an unvoiced refrain to chatty surface dialogue.

10

Now, we were mid-river, from the bridge, no guarding wall,
a moment we floated, could see northward and southward
the sacred waterway, vast, it called out for the land to sink
into slow turbulence. But crossed, hit the other shore's green
left the dun pulsations behind. A smooth four-laner opened
before us, sparsely trafficked; the interstate way-home wove
between limestone knolls. The Steam Boat passengers flitted
through my driving concentration while we were storm-riding.
And your friend picked up the hidden theme, gazed elsewhere,
said aloud, 'I wouldn't want to be out in the river in this', as if
we'd followed a narrative from beginning to end, then stopped.
Lightning stabbed, incandescent streaks, bomb-flashes right,
cannon-cracker thunderclaps, sprinkled drops on windshield.
We were on the run; pushing grey areas beyond the speed limit.
Then ahead we sighted a car in the ditch, in the big green divide
between dual lanes, gently nose-down. On the westward lane
stopped, state police, red & blue flashing, in afternoon's night.

Passing the scene conversation re-awoke: about slippery roads'
treachery, especially after a long dry spell. You carried the gist
all the way back to your near fatal crash on a British curve —
against the rules you'd slammed breaks and of nature you
didn't slide across but spun round, till facing the way back.
'If the car had hit me on the driver's side I would be dead...'
That panic spin saved you. I didn't dwell on escapology.
Brooded that you might not have been here, sat alongside,
sometimes your hand on my thigh, then fiddling with a vent,
in this cockpit (us never meeting) what way to have gone then?
Near death experiences after the smash, shook out your life.
In back, your friend, call her sister, a widow, she bore her
recent dead, a husband, lifelong protector, apple tree farmer
a functionalist with a knack for knowing when the itinerant
workers were around for pruning (she'd earlier said) when
to act before leaves were shot-holed. What did she think?...
The back's hush near tangible as you unpeeled your story.
I grasped the steering wheel with both slack hands; wipers
sluiced the silly fall, as if this thunder stuff was histrionics.

11

We crossed once more the Illinois, panoramic, the river asleep
between brawny greens that looked never-to-be-encroached-on.
We left the main route and followed river valley's edge north,
the byway meandered to contours. An instinct arose. We had
to stop, find higher ground, to view the spectacle in the west.
Climbed a gravel lane on the right to a hill-patched cemetery.
Your pal blushed, 'strange, but I have never noticed it before.'
Our desire for an instant viewpoint ('before the scene changed'
you'd nudged) led us to a wall-less field's exposed emotions.
There'd be no one-way watching. My heart pulled the other.
They looked recent stones, in a freshly delved burying yard.
We idled with the dead and they placed their counterweight
on everything we saw and imagined. Among that near throng
a US flag waved, near ground level, a baby flag on a plot,

blue and white on a stick that a child might shake at a parade.
I suspected a soldier's last-rest. We zoomed windows down,
let a coarse breeze in with its sulphurous gunpowder smell.
We each took our different vantage. I saw black mountain-
stolid cloud, valleys cut from a concealed ball's laser beams.
Lower, sky had a grey lid that the sun looked ready to pry off
in a second. Then rain filed down. We muttered, closed in glass.
It drummed a wild man on the roof, a panicked military tattoo.
I turned the motor, the hood nosed toward our short-stay home
in muted response. In the distance, our morning's suspension
bridge glittered — a stretched spider web on the prairie horizon.

12

The day's savage grace had not reached its end. We swung
into a minor, no white bandages down its middle or white lines
along its shoulder, the road narrowed or widened on a whim.
I remembered a tale — a near-blind driver who was allowed
his licence under the pretext that his car knew the way home —
like a saddled horse through the man's familiar districts.
I thought maybe I'd gaze stunned like my fellow travellers
just let the car propel himself. The sun threw off its grey
hood, shot out intense rays making each raindrop a prism
sending off a vast, then double, arc with iridescent colours
across the black, due east sky, as if twin bridges of hope
that the Ancient Mariner, or a prairie schooner could pass
below, the strongest rainbow, its whole underside silvered.
We seemed aimed there, pursuing legends into that space.

13

Suddenly, from lank shadowed corn stalks, a deer charged
leaped across our head beams. We'd slowed to 20, 15 mph.
It was white or brown, who could say? It darted, crossing
the road at full tilt, kept its footing on the greasy surface,

fled across bare earth, into an opposite field, then woods.
A moment's utter recognition between us three, then gone,
you retold a primal memory: how with your dad, in your
Kentish garden, you'd first seen a double spanned bow.

14

Much later, I stood outside your friend's farmhouse,
tubular chimes rattled on the screened-in verandah.
I leaned against one of her trees (you'd gone to bed).
She had known you so much, so much longer than me.
I forgot what creatures might slither, slide between
my wet feet. She'd reassured, 'the snakes are mostly
down at the creek'. In complete darkness, I studied
the lightning that jittered along soot and ash margins,
the storm's aftermath. The barn owls were sheltering.
The tornado hinted sky ignited with jagged capillaries,
like a body turned inside out. Every clouds' inners
exposed; closed up, then pulled apart in an autopsy.
I wished that you were by me, watching this: young
again, before I knew you, able to stand any weather.
Listened for the following thunder, counted seconds
but each time reached crazy figures against retained
silence as another scented breeze stirred her orchard.
Only after an extreme display could I make out above
some cough, a hollowed reply. I turned back toward
the dim house: Mississippi and its nation, way behind.

Her Apple Tree Farm

A memoir of Illinois

I

The first Crab's amethyst
through a screen verandah —
'for the flowers' she says.

A tweeting not yet airborne
among loud lengthening sweeps —
veteran evergreens

Sat on her silky bronze
needle floor — we three savour
a heaped crisp salad lunch.

A red fish creating
swells through green ocean —
a Cardinal in flight

Her gravel drive's dry
where two blue-eyed Grackles met
and splashed yesterday.

In the bed Abraham
Lincoln slept, I half doze —
'a train's God-fearing hoot.'

Johnny Appleseed —
ahead of the steam frontier
planted his nurseries

First Nations loved him
the pale skin who made
the valleys flamboyant

Vachel Lindsay spoke
poems to share in his landscape's
mythical breathing.

You and I sneak off —
during a prairie downpour.
One mines her orchard...

she'll nurse the seasons —
red-white blooms to ruby fruit —
back round to infinity.

II

Fate might be displaced among slumped branches narrowing orchard lanes. A bee laces blossoms like fastening ribbons of a bonnet. The owner tells me about the king bud with his surrounding attendants. If the head is fertilised, not cut off by rain or frost, you have a big apple. If the king dies, the cornet of little buds might produce a family of small apples. But one or many must be lost. A huge Red Delicious symbol stands in relief on the garage's white front, below the triangular roof beyond the tractor with flattened tyres; its diesel funnel rusted.

What is the passion I absorb walking, ducking under flower profuse limbs, no longer pruned, but allowed freedom? If I see a racer snake disguised among budding networks would be unable to tell the difference, so stroll cautious, drag my feet through untrimmed grass. In these parts that fear of an attacker. Not satisfied my nervousness comes from snakes. From where does a death threat emerge? Flowering limbs need the right-weather-balance to be fulfilled and not abandoned and disgraced. How does anxiety and passion relate? What prevails to be passionate about? Spring is maturing as it should towards heat and silence when blossoms fall and summer's practice of growing goes on, the outward diminishing, the inward expanding.

The orchard didn't look this way from an airliner's porthole, patterned trees begged attention among vast open stretches. Now they hardly want to notice my steps. Maybe it's John Chapman's (1774-1845) steps the orchard hears, who planted the seeds in Vachel Lindsay's (1879-1931) phrase 'Heart of a hundred midnights, heart of the merciful morns. / Heaven's boughs bent down with their alchemy.' Can myth and the man walk side by side? One dying like 'a stone washed white' the other living in each apple, in monuments and human memory?

Two lovers, on the underground-railroad, have slipped under branches, disappeared into the land's closure while a voice rose from somewhere calling them back to the homestead, to believe in a verandah's smallness; its wooden columns wanting white paint strokes. May be not a human utterance but a crow's caw, finch's chitterling, a dove's coo-cooing. The two were carrying all they owned, escaping, their hands inside each other's, grasping future as the past hunted. Didn't know if they would find what they were told would shelter and guide, (what house to turn back towards?) The couple couldn't be sure. That twosome didn't dread snakes.

I don't reckon them, pressing through, in mid-afternoon. Not fearing sound of my swishing passage. Be loud. Not them. Someone might know. Their eyes dark or blue sweeping green growth, marvelling at liberty, its encroaching conclusion, being one step ahead, make no mistakes, take no wrong turns, keep from your own kind. Don't bash king buds, walk bowed, un-disturbing the sleepers, quiet let no alarm summon people to enquire who's weaving a route between landmarks. There's no way. Their fate to arrive where they received food, drink and good will. So hesitant, careful they moved not wanting to trouble a butterfly or honey bee. Take nothing from the land, but freedom, travel on secretly, through convoluted groves.

I don't see them. Rustle of predicted leaves; who's walking? Maybe they see me, have been watching, to be trusted or avoided, vacillate if they'll need to ambush or can let me pass but hope I'll stumble, won't move; they, that fear and love, walk with whole passions, and maybe hope I'll trip, be bitten by a poisonous snake. If there's a victim, they can pass unharmed.

Which door to knock on? Window to stare through? Is that friendly barking or aggressive? Stay away, among Johnny Appleseed boughs. Don't trust anyone. Walk earth-rivers. Am I a victim or victimiser? I'm innocent, what should happen? Why an inner fervour when nothing should? Is the weather changing, big and small buds threatened? Storm's massacre. Every escapee captured, killed. Cloud armies moving on, crushing grass, smashing. Or is it a plague?

That president, Abraham Lincoln, lived near. Had to go east to power-battles, to civil war and assassination. A birdsong's caution. I sleep in his bed, some say, curved walnut carved with plain design, head-stead echoes the foot, (beginning and end the same) a long sleeping couch, where the slumber-er is near to leaping up, engaging in paper at a built-in desk. He had to go east to big cities, warring politics; he didn't return to apple trees. Could he have stayed, helped pass on underground lovers to the next clearing a house surrounded by pine and shrubs like an outpost? What then? He gave a farewell address, got on a train; travelled with big motives.

Did death have bigger motives? Is it coiling round trees? Once someone's died among the flora scented air, can it be ousted, must it remain to discomfort whoever passes through, no matter a century or more on? I'm not haunted or in a hurry but something impassions. Look back, to the side, the land pitches toward a gully where a stream digs into brown-black soil. Can't see the way I've come. Not lost, in the normal sense. I almost observe the house's whiteness through blurs of long needled white pines; then it's gone. No house. Destroyed sometime, a half filled foundation, bit of rubble, grassed over, sunken, with scattered rotten floor boards. I nearly spy its proportioned windows, its chimney and wood-pillar verandah sloping. The ground subsides from train-shaking and fate's high-stepping tramp. Death's still younger than those fleeing lovers, quieter, un-detained among brightening branches, like fate.

Don't sit under the apple tree
with anyone else but me.

Chapin, Illinois, USA

Stopping at Schenectady, New York

Once a Boom Town
Day One

From the grand 1920s' house
I hear melting snow flip-flop
from a wrap-round porch roof.

Inside: down the banister perches
an ornamental red cardinal —
once ravaged by a cat.

For breakfast: Swiss pancakes,
sliced peach and morsels of sausages
cased in maple syrup.

Outside: the city's a ghost town.
I'm told outlying malls
have abducted the shoppers.

In the Nott Memorial — a Pope's glass hat —
the dark domed ceiling glitters in red-amber,
mauve and azure — a Blake's galaxy.

For lunch Cajun food:
cornbread and Jambalaya
in the Melo Joy Café.

Up, a profusion of mugs
swing from wall pegs, tempting
customers to reach highest.

In the town's Stockade District
lintels and shutters
resist embellishment.

The first evening, my B&B hostess picks up
my query, portrays the city's decline,
side-steps her own sorrow.

A sign propped on a table reads:
'Don't worry about switching
the light off — it's on a timer.'

City of Light
Day Two

Edison's adopted
Schenectady
lately feels disowned.

Still this look of normalcy —
the out of work thousands
dissolve into shabby facades.

Masks of abandonment
across corroded gates
and gawking windows.

Some citizens attempt
revival, to rekindle
a quenched urban flame.

My breakfast sequel:
Eggs Benedict
and Pumpkin Cake,

the house-carer concludes,
'Done my particular way'

her each sentence ends
played-down with a humbling 'so'

she almost sings a da-da-da
in the middle of her melody.
Ambitions, outside,
huge factories, palatial Post Office
for a city forecast to succeed.

Over an intersection
like good-luck charms
stop-lights bob.

Big Erie Boulevard
follows the inner city route
the Erie Canal once travelled.

I'm in a general store stroking
cuddly Beanies — this year's rage — not sure
handling the merchandise
is A OK around here.

Monster veranda homes (1920s)
stand back from Union Street;
divided-down in Camelot sixties;
refurbished c. 1990s as in vogue B&Bs.

Back indoors: my hostess is hard to find then
our paths cross and she oozes accommodation

'help yourself, if you want anything
from the fridge or the sideboard bowl.'

What's it like to live in this
huge guest house alone?

Second evening's words curtailed
her 'goodnight' lacks a retreating glance.

Over her mantel-piece a frame shows-off
a picket-fence homestead so out of scale
with the foreground's decorative cattle.

In a comfy alcove —
a model village emits light
its street-lamps gilded.

A Venue like a City
Day Three

Out of hours
I enter the Proctor Theatre.
The manageress enthuses
'You want to see it? I'll get the key.'

She boosts:
'Two thousand and seven hundred red seats.
Look at the oval ceiling, the re-shone chandelier.'
more involved than rococo.

She starts again:
'Finished 1926… vaudeville…
then rapid decline.'

'One day I met off the plane, George Burns.
So frail he might've expired right there
at ninety-five. It's here he gave
his last performance.'

She keeps bumping my shoulder
catching my arm, drawing me in
'I love this place'.

She guides under frolicking
stucco through shadows made
by curlicue balconies.

No rectangles: seats, ceiling and walls curved,
long, climbing aisles swerve with pleasure.

A Pleasure House, A Music Hall I muse,
imagine exotic acts applauded,
her fingers tap-dance down my sleeve.

She leads into a dressing-room, we taste
the oldness, the promiscuity,
she flicks the lights off and leaves.

She's right to be quick.
I could happily ravish her
in one of these George Burns'
dressing-rooms on a long sofa.

Bulbs brocade the make-up mirror,
white fluffs on the floor
that a draught cannot move.

'This bigger room,' her voice slows
'was the chorus line's.'

'Come! You must see the stage,
see the place from the front
looking back at the audience.'

I'm a stand-in peering out, waiting
for the ovation. In stage-fright

I turn, see the stage's dark extent
with so many backdrops.

Its row of great up-winding ropes
that lower and hoist
depending on the hour's drama.

Her attention remains pinned to the apron.
'A ghost-light,' she informs.

Without a shade, one of Edison's bulbs
is held erect on top a black stem — a filamented bud.

Ghost, I echo.
What does that mean?
On cue we speculate.

She claims: 'It keeps the ghosts away.'
Drifting across the stage, I puzzle which:
past loves, last night's bad performance,
a poor house, decades of decline?

The venue starts to look grotesque.
She finds a tighter adjective
'Looks theatrical.'

Then soliloquies
'For people experienced as yourself and me
things are different.'

I have no idea from which raised drop
her words have unfurled like a curtain.

Guessing my spin
she tucks at my inside cuff
and leads me to the sprawling lobby.

'Schmaltzy' she reforms
my impression to keep me in step
with her burlesque viewpoint.

Sticking a show-biz kiss on her cheek,
'That's nice,' she wisps at the tour's end.

Closing Act
Day Four

Waiting to board the Amtrak
westbound, I review how much will-power
excited her loving face.

Around the raised platform,
with little history to hide behind,
assorted costumes and spectacles
of the depressed city
stand exposed.

Across open ground, some citizens
have set out to preserve
the glitzy sign script
on the brick forehead
of a derelict plant.

A line of George Burns —
on the theme of leaving —
clicks, shuffles and leaps through...
his black shoes shiny as the rails
before my train arrives.

Canada — America

The train swings out along
Lake Ontario's shore
over bridged bays and inlets,
past once busy harbours
long silted into marsh, past
Jordan and Dalhousie that seem
to re-emerge, a thousand white wings
across the still open water's grey.

Passing acres of small naked trees,
a veteran conductress reveals
she loves to travel this route in spring
when from both sides, blossoms
white and pink overtake the orchards.

Next stop Niagara Falls!
Honeymoon capital of the world
she might've once crooned.

Against a Canadian-facing window
a passenger, crunched under her fur-lapel coat,
glances around, like me travelling alone.
A red and blue pom-pom, as if a parting corsage,
fastened to the grip of her big, weathery case.

Crossing the Niagara has never been easier,
the primal river's reduced to a leapable gush.

The train slows, squealing to rest in the border-zone.
U. S. customs officers step on board,
decorated with badges sublime as the Falls,
and dark-handled guns.
Just the facts, ma'am
requires a vintage Dragnet detective.

The U. S. recognises one citizenship only,
states the official from his navy windbreaker,
disowning each hyphened nationality.

Out the stationary window
rusted sumac tops
and purple of wild raspberry canes
sway madly similar
to those on the other side.
Pearl necklaces
like contraband
embellish the glass.

Yesterday, in a downtown gift-store,
I peered hard into each jewellery case.
Excuse me, a female stranger
held up two objects
for inspection, *You're a man,*
which of these rings do you think
my husband would prefer?

After an irritating delay —
tracks from custom's vehicles
having left decorative arcs —
the train starts to edge forward, wheels
screeching toward the next arrival call.

At breakfast, my mother mentioned her travels
during the thirties' to New York City:
an excited young girl peering out
the family car's rear side-window.
Slowing up at some lights a youth leapt
from nowhere on to the running board.
Cars had running boards then, mum inserted.
The boy hollered, *Got somewhere to stay?*
No! the joint answer. He grinned widely,
clutched a door handle, fixed his feet to rubber tread,

hanging on in Keystone Cop style, directed
the family to a nice clean hotel off Times Square.
She spoke as if perplexed by that outcome.
Him receiving from her dad a five-star tip.

States-side, back then, Canadian plates were rare.
During prohibition, a New Yorker fooled,
Haven't you guys smuggled some drink?
What other reason to tour dry America?
In another adventure, I was told, the family
obediently followed an AAA map into Harlem
and after a crazy day ended up begging for sleep.
OK! the hotelier finally conceded,
I guess we can sneak a few whities in.

At last we stutter into Buffalo.
Between railway cars, brash rain splashes
turning to indeterminate snow.
As again the locomotive gains speed
I enter a conversation with an American
who begins almost at once
to trace his Italian Irish roots.
My grandfather was murdered
in 1917. Killed in a village one night
in the Virginia coalfields, him and three others.

No immigrant's grave. Barbed wire pulled tight
round a tree marked where he'd died.
Grandmother, still carrying my father,
was a witness. The truth never came out.
I came back, years on, and saw a bulge
where the trunk had grown over his straps of iron.

Across the café car's arbourite table
my fellow traveller stares away
then asserts, *I'm licensed to carry a firearm.*

I never draw out my gun as a threat,
only to kill. Far ahead the train hoots
a protracted warning
moaning onwards, 'Look out, Look out'
as a night flying bird's impassioned call.

I watch those brisk customs guards
with their black, polished revolvers
and I want to snatch the brute from its holster,
point the snout in their faces — reverse
that power — claim my right to self-annihilation.

Nearly all passengers have changed.
I glimpse in the shivering glass, myself writing
as if somehow getting to the bottom of it.
Frail winter orchards stretch back
toward a beginning blacked-out.
Remember, I should phone home when I arrive.

Through space, a tunnel's opened
as if, in a precognitive way, to see the unseen,
one more long drawn out hoot's expelled
toward Rochester, followed by Syracuse, on to Albany.

Lights flashing by grow remote as stars, until
between them and me, I imagine a cosmos.
My mother's journeys down New York State,
in her father's car, were glossed by a quest
for discovery: that kept the Rockefeller Centre,
Street Arabs, Empire State and '39 World Fair
on a human scale; made her dreams approachable.

At home, without a conspicuous illness,
she declines bit by bit toward a lesser
and lesser here and now, from which
there's no return, just as gran once claimed.

One day in the car, of herself and dad, mum said,
We're shrinking.... Repeated the phrase—
I felt their expanding absence.

Through moisture-leaden night the horn
sounds and resounds; keeps surfacing.
When my destination is reached the train's
clicketty clack and prolonged hooting goes on.
Over a relaxed dinner, as a new dialogue starts
I attempt once more to find an image for that
arresting call... its abstruse, repetitive sounding-out.

Lincolnshire, A New Millennium

'Crossing the Bar'

A Gift from Granddad

I stare into your gift, like a well,
trusting to see your reflection.
You took Tennyson's poem
printed on flimsy card, you
mounted, glazed and framed it.
You were a poet and craftsman
and with your artisan skill
made it look like art.

I can't remember when you
pressed it into my hands
to be valued forever.
It was before leaving my homeland.
I re-read the Laureate's words.
You loved his old style rhyming
but used straightforward speaking
when I was about to embark:
'We come into this world alone
and alone we'll leave it.'

I look longingly at your object,
the discolouring, foxing on
both sides and above the title
like beauty spots, growing old
somehow beautifies the thing
and makes it almost secret —
no longer a universal poem
but an intimate reminder.

Grandpa, you offered this memento
so perhaps in time I would recall
that in youth you were my pilot

when I was eager to throw every-
thing away you chose subtly a poem
about death to re-inspire me with life,
to be a benchmark I should aim for.

You've been gone forty years and still
I miss your directing hand and sense.

I stare too long through the clear
sheet, past fancy script, into depths
trying to imagine you, to conjure
some moment we shared in trust
as a grandfather and grandson can.
And yet, your see-through glass
deceives, it merely reflects back me
and my preparation and crossing
from this world; not so far ahead.
You, no doubt, expected your gift
would have that purpose some hour
when passing it on like a heirloom.
It had helped you. It will help me.

Somersby

'I prosper, circled with thy voice'
ALFRED LORD TENNYSON

Following a ploughed over Roman road
I find Somersby and walk close-round
its grassy church, half read inscriptions.
I know no one in young Tennyson's home.
A red kiosk stands by a shy girl's yard gate
and beside the field a tractor, its engine off,
from the cab a two-way radio chattering on.
I approach the old rectory: maybe invited in
to stroll through the poet's childhood rooms
and corridors, find a whiff from musky walls.
But my civil knocks pass unnoticed. The older
Tennyson, among dazzling imperial tributes,
read *In Memoriam* to his jet-shawled Queen.
The way into here, and the way out, follow
the cultivation's contours as if everything fits
in this hamlet as if an empire could relax
in the cupped palm of his unexotic hills.

Lincoln Vignettes

for B.H

Through green's varied age
you and I step, butterflies rampant
on the Witham's slithering bank

Purple, lead-black
elderberries bridge
a small opening

Ivy graces
broken red brick outcrops
along the brownish
greying river

Adolescent boys lean back and cast
above the rusted sluice gate
show off to passing girls

Single file children
tempting river nymphs
stroll along the flood barrier wall

Topping Lindum hill
the carnivalesque cathedral
on view

Suddenly sun-lit,
the city's a stained glass mosaic —
canals and overflow dykes dividing

Wheels up!
a dumped superstore trolley
appears above the Witham's flow

In formation
cygnets and adults stroke
through the arched Glory Hole

Curved like a long-bow
a sea-weathered bow pushes out
the canal curls back, gleaming

A vivacious captain
in a pied coloured dress
handles the metal-bare tiller

The pilot poised
an infant sways in his lap
scarlet looping his neck.

Perhaps: the youngest
family of three
steering toward open water

You tell me:
from Brayford
you pictured how the voyage out
might have been
robed in Victorian sails.

from The Glory Hole Project

she remembers
they last met here
where the open
water narrows

she forgets
they last embraced
where the open water
narrows

I can't tell
from this side
whether that glance
calls me or not

clandestine invaders
lifting their ocean-blades

here, a nation stepped on board
with no destination
in this world

an airman's wings
squadron of mallards
safely splash down

a synchronised splash
squadron of mallards land

down, a squadron of mallards skids
she remembers an airman's wings

squadron of mallards skid-down
she remembers her boyfriend's wings

someone must grip
the tiller of the whole world
through its darkest hour

Swans on the Witham

After the deluge
in an island's lee adults loiter

ingathering a naive gaze
a grey cygnet manoeuvres

inky Brayford Pool a solo mute
writes *Spring* upon it

white necks snaking down
to graze the bottom green

through a blizzard midstream
past midnight two piloting

another day toward the Glory Hole
small heads in the clouds

phenomenal creatures steer and glide
noon-light plating feathers and tall necks

air vibrates like a kettledrum
white fluffs on the jade canal

capsized in shallows, wings create
a cradle for vestiges of down

one leans its head to greet
foot-falls on strident stairs

wings stripped to splintered quills
St Hugh's bird glides by.

The Bridge at Midnight

They were few. They were many. They stumbled
and dragged their belongings down stone steps,
saw the tunnel to a far harbour and listened to
the water's slow rise. They had to board, feel
the anchor among a people who hated them,
who called them forward by cursing names,
pleased and determined to see them banished.
They had to creak up a gangway under torches,
pretend they were nothing but passing shadows
among ship-hands who believed they were child-
killers, who defiled young girls, and had betrayed
a nation's trust, trading away its gold. They had to
pay above the odds, at a dead hour, set sail — not
knowing where the dark river would carry them.

Holy Week Sequence
(excerpts)

Why, disciples ask,
Toward Rome's Jerusalem,
To where you are loathed?

Sunday Before

Ochre earth's sterile season.
   Yet forsythia and daffodils quake
      as if welcoming palms.

After Vesper
   hyacinth fragrance seems diffused
      through vineyard parable.

Monday

Those uninscribed vistas
   the grief of Time and Space: who can discern
      a universal sorrow?

Or from the celebratory crowd
   hold their gaze on that human figure
      edging toward death?

Unageingly intimate,
   unblinded by the site or the hour,
      He intuits finality.

Nor was transfiguration
   a closure, but the prelude to His Voice
      announcing Awake.

A woman, outside, wonders;
  thin, crossed arms, with inflexible grip,
    shielding her victim's heart.

From the savaged tree,
  but subdued, to the deflating afternoon sky,
    a blackbird whistles.

Tuesday

That estranged night-shift, prolonged.
  Garbed with the sun a worker comes home,
    vanquished at daybreak.

Sparse green hawthorn twigs
  with infant-tenderness
    embrace a twisted-iron fence.

Intrepid, Christ stood
  among them — arguing from their text —
    portraying His peace.

Her bulged, black-and-blued right eye,
  a passing woman glares straight ahead
    repulsing a stranger's glance.

Deep, yellow-centred,
  a purple primrose has bloomed
    with love-shaped petals.

Wednesday

Before Christ suffered:
  smooth fingertips, as he relaxed,
    perfumed his body.

Dark coat-ends fly up!
  A black rook, through sheeting rain,
    lifts into violence.

Green, as red, splattered,
  along the broken vista briars bleed,
    crudely severed.

Far from Tuesday's wrangles
  on an evening hill his disciples heard Infinity's gasp,
    Night's coda.

Holy Thursday

At this terminal world's nightfall
  less dramatic clouds unleash
    darkness's deluge

Sleep on! night-watchers.
  Pressed to earth, your Lord, Bread and Wine,
    prays the nux animae pass...

He's long known can never.
  From nocturnal height to a new, demented dawn
    rain strikes! lashes! beats!

Twilight's franticness
  foretells an absolute moon:
    each extreme attained.

Good Friday

Flecked with white flowers
  the maroon tree turns scarlet —
    beyond life's window.

Soldiers stand jeering, mocking.
   As shook in numberless fists
      coins and keys jangle.

Christ's anguish of love,
   for which, He was Spirit-conceived,
      died as though disowned.

Hate and fear overwhelmed:
   who can wrestle back Amor's triumph?
      Serenely, God's prince rests.

His corpse, they prepared
   with essences; then wrapped in cere-bands
      as rocks cried, *Our Lord!*

Holy Saturday

Agape, a small book
   stares up from the table's frayed cloth
      among scattered crumbs.

He grapples with Night,
   like a moon into black-massing cloud
      till he re-appears.

Without a footprint's weight,
   He undertakes His intractable journey:
      vanished. All Life mourns.

The garden, the cave, sleeps.
   The cosmic battle-ground concealed.
      On this Sabbath; the sky's fireless.

From death's stranglehold
  He loosens the maimed, the once-murdered,
    the long lost, naive, the sacrificed.

Watchful pilgrims desire
  the world's Logos to return
    One God to ascend.

Easter Sunday

Taciturn, benighted,
  who quests so early through fragrant green-tips
    for the Chosen Dawn?

Quiet heads under closed wings,
  guarding the path, as though quions,
    two mallards repose.

Dawn-scarfed, at her gate,
  the first ageless widow acclaims
    her gardener's care.

Spring's chaotic torment:
  what can allay it except the Love
    that can never ebb?

She weeps: but for whom?
  Across that unending concealment
    the smallest bird has trilled.

Stunned, first mourners stand back.
  The gigantic stone's shifted.
    Astounded ether sings...

Servant, Survivor
  out-breathing fate, who redeems sorrow,
    One suffering Rock.

In patience instructing,
  in Love as through the beatitudes, in Faith as peace
    and Hope as wisdom.

Our own substratum
  can we not address: to that abandonment bring
    a tendon of human light?

The star's intimate labour accomplished.
  So fiercely earned, the Messiah's death-clothes lie.
    Soft: Christ greets a friend.

What more, my Saviour,
who died for me? I died too.
My risen one, am I you?

My Love, do not touch.
O touch, as I touch, from one God
through all time, all space.

*

Why, disciples ask,
toward Rome's Jerusalem,
to where you are loathed.

Long Sutton Day

Church bells spanked the summer sky. From the library five of us set out walking through a hot Saturday, coated in sun block lotion. In front of St Mary's, a VW wedding. As honour guard, veteran cars were lined up decorated with blue and white streamers; the bride and groom passionate about the people's car. From shop doorways, many on this cloudless morning stared. A motorcar from that era needed special grooming and preparation to stand out in the sun and show off in front of a crowd, not unlike the young bride and groom. We admired and walked on toward the Fens' level fields. Five, my partner Barbara and I, and Holly, Sally and Jo, the latter sisters, Holly a play-group leader; all much younger than us two and quicker a foot.

At a corner we passed a Sailor Boy Charity Shop. The sea, in these parts is the great land-shaker: feared orphan-maker. Not a whiff of offshore breeze, hint of fish smell reached my nose that I worried might burn off, applying more lotion. The present North Sea and Wash had long retreated, chased by intervention and ingenuity that pushed back lilting waves and drained the fens, turning them into fecund enclosed acres. Silting, too, part of the history. We came to a road called Roman Bank; on the map traced an old coastline. We crossed and took our first steps, beyond outcrops of houses, into the imaginary sea: up to our necks, then over our heads, sub-mariners, bathing in the heat, walking on ground begging for water. Pausing, the reclaimed land inspired us in different ways, each with our private notebook, jotted. We greeted a farmer, strolling toward us rolling with sweat, who said, 'You all look busy'.

buoy in violent sea,
bell of St Mary's
out across the fen.

Our way followed a narrow uneven path, dangerous in a wet-season, tricky at any time. Flora overlaid the privet hedgerow that shadowed our watchful steps by an extending wheat field.

out of season
for wild rose — wild clematis
plays the part.

Through the hedge water glimmered. I consulted the leaflet. Jo
and Sally, knowing the area, said, almost in unison, they were
surprised to find a pond here. The pond's rim appeared haphazard
as if its creation, an accident. I explained it was the area's last
clay pit. A straggly tree clung to the reflective bank as if it had an
undisclosed purpose. Again, we wrote. Our walk, a creative writing
workshop on the hoof; each narrating shared but separate day's
journey. I questioned if anyone had noted that willow, so different
I figured, than Bashō's Japanese willow, from whose hanging
shade he stepped, three centuries ago, and heard the women's rice-
planting songs. That's what was absent here: the people — workers,
farmers, harvesters and planters — that made the land hum with
produce. Was it summer heat or the style of agriculture? Gazing
from sky to earth, Holly tended to lag, her pen moved over small
bound pages. We strolled on, careful where we placed our feet on
hardened, pot-holed roasted soil. According to Edward Storey, the
poet John Clare made regular excursions into the lowland 'where
the great clouds on the horizon became his only mountains'. Yet
'Clare's publishers and friends could not understand how he ever
found inspiration in this dull landscape.' The same disbelief was
stated about Tennyson and his local terrain of Wolds and Fens. Our
quintet of writers looked well-inspired by the level land on all sides
around us.

a ballpoint wiggles
from an amazed walker's grip —
flies down to the path.

the wind's arid
combing voice
speaks through aspens.

Day hours advanced. Sail-less wind increased. Holly described its sound as water bursting down a mountainside. I thought, Niagara, my Canadian homeland, conjuring images of Queenston Heights, above a turquoise Gorge. Often, I noticed out of the side of my eye, my partner and Holly in conversations from which a stranded word or phrase escaped. Sally and I talked about the growing season, how green was lengthening over years, frosted winters squeezed into childhood recollections: her and Jo from a nearby farming background. Holly from Cambridgeshire, so she knew Waterlands and the fens; Barbara, from the Midlands, had spent hers in the north of England. She had stories about nights in Nottingham and trials of getting home, catching the last bus, running full tilt. For me the fens were alien landscape. I had scraps of information, picked up from Hidden Lincolnshire and Waterside Walks that referred to the Peter Scott Way, I imagined must be not far toward Sutton Bridge and River Nene. His patronage opened the land for the public. His concern for environment, his art, brought conservationist legacy to the Wash and cargo-groaning estuaries, to coned lighthouses above encroaching marshes, where brunette flash of reed warblers comes and goes.

We threaded along margins of a sugar beet fields. Barbara with poetic licence called them 'sugar fields' setting off connotations in my sun-logged brain. The harsh almost bitter land, overworked and controlled, was freed and sweetened. Between gigantic fields, green wilderness strips prevailed. We held for each other rebellious limbs that shot across the path. The undergrowth rustled with blackberries, nettles and Cow Parsley, that Jo pointed to as 'architectural'. Radials of bronze wilted heads ascended into blue. The border of aspen, oak, poplar and grey-leafed sycamore, stiffly sang, calling my heart to four compass points.

Peter Scott could've hiked
this way — wheat as tall
under forget-me-not blue.

flies burr round
a dead vole, red blotches
no longer oozing.

We moved slowly by a potato landscape. Along bare ridges, haulms
stood brunt and draggled. Out of sight, pulpy fruit ripened on
underground branches. Jo said farmers spray potatoes to make
tops die-off quicker. Growers apologise for the burning smell
that arises, she added; but no odour invaded, just a look of rank
devastation, as if after a Danish long-boat raid, the terrain scorched.
Invaders couldn't hold marginal land where many Saxons found
refuge among holmes or islands, again finding sanctuary after
the Norman victory at Hastings. Dark potato fields subdued us, I
speculated on what each co-walker recorded. Industry has been
exaggerated long before drainage schemes, previous inhabitants
hunted waterfowl with nets covering an acre and guns as long as
punting poles. Other businesses pressed in, hired guides showed
routes across treacherous lowlands. Northern cattle, fattened on
thick grasses, pushed on to London markets, across land-bridges;
their legacy left in the derivative Drove. Nomadic men led
centuries of cattle herds. Mothers kept young ones from the racket
and wildness of hooves; today they stop their children getting close
to stampeding cars and lorries on the A17.

drifter clouds
far above where thousands
of droves crossed.

Now and then, I looked for 17th century graves that I'd read
about. in *Land, People and Landscape*. Simple designed, hardly a
foot above ground, cut in oolite, with no spaces between Roman
capitalised words of name, date and location. Their displayed
humility occupied as I walked by a waterless dyke. The immense
sugar-beet and potato-fields died out; on the right bowed heads of
bold wheat addressed us. Over the dyke we crossed a millennium
bridge, a few strong planks, a wooden railing on one side.
Overgrown and near collapse after two years. Along banks

smothering the dried out watercourse, wildflowers — gipsywort, convolvulus and bogbean (I wasn't sure of their names), sent up a whiff of perfume. Then, from the chatter, someone pointed to a ground-cover of small, concave, translucent disks.

pink bindweed
like my grandmother's
rarely used china.

From England she immigrated to Canada, a breath from World War I, with her husband to be. The Salvation Army assisted passage. She paid off the debt a chore-girl in Halifax, while grandfather travelled another two thousand miles to Hamilton seeking work in carpentry. She had fled the Old World, dropped her life, and rushed to the New with little idea of what might be encountered... with a man she'd met on Brighton Pier. Her first disappointment, their enforced separation. He land-locked; she stranded in port. Distant decencies and bitterness was imprinted in bindweed rows and tilted series of side-plates behind glass that I recalled. Unusually we weren't strung out, but bunched up, following a flyblown track, crunching gravel under-toes, testing ourselves on names of flora. I eager to catch from a phrase a new species or language-use. Then the women collected, looking over a spread of white-hearted yellows, like a coverlet. Fever-few, they agreed. Barbara gave me a leaf. Pungent crushed in the hand. 'It has set itself', Jo said. I sighted on the side a sheaf of poppies and scribbled:

November
remembrances
among boldest wheat

In the 1970s when my English-born grandparents both died, my craftsman soldier-father wanted to make a plaque to place above their graves, but the authorities wouldn't let him. We stepped along the unbending bridleway, no hummocks hid the view; the land level as I imagined the Wash's sea-bed, that the ancients, to medieval times, ferried across from Marsh to Norfolk. The country's eastern side was the centre; Lincoln and Boston, the kingdom's second cathedral, a string of monasteries and a port. Abbeys and wool diminished, the harbour silted. In the Fens holy men, like St Guthlac, found isolated islets ('could be occupied without dispossessing a previous owner') and in seclusion practiced their devotion to God until they became famous and were sought by kings seeking counsel. To the thirteen century scholar William of Malmesbury the Fens were 'a very paradise and a heaven for the beauty and delight thereof, the very marshes bearing goodly trees... such abundance of fish.' In later centuries, the centre of the land and commerce shifted toward Nottingham, civil government and later, the industrial Midlands. The road and railway went through Newark, bridging the Trent, Lincolnshire became marginalised. This mentality of 'being out on a limb' from then on developed: not from geographical disadvantage, but history's tireless momentum of change.

Heat biting, we struggled on. No-one turned back. Barbara questioned, leaning on my shoulder, 'Do you know the way?' Up ahead, by the track, stood a shed. Utilitarian as the Second World War. Jo and Sally peered at the corrugated roof, inspected the interior through grimy windows. It could be a drying shed, a place farm-workers slept during harvest. Why should a drying shed have windows? I didn't debate. Puzzled, searching through the panes; I mulled over who curled-up sleepers might have been on a straw-bedded floor. Our conversation turned to immigrants, itinerants this empty landscape conceals. Who were they? Who transformed the land? The Dutch came, built drains, sluice gates; they left their culture in names, South Holland, Kesteven, in architecture of houses steep rooved with curvy red-brick gables. 'At least they had food', Sally or Jo interrupted my stream. The Irish came to work. They knew there was toil, food and shelter on the fens — now, it's Afrikaans. I hear, they use the Internet in Sutton Library, without a word of English. People think this region's mono-cultural. It's full of different nationalities. The Irish would've returned to their homeland on a 'double-passage' back to crofts or tenements. Now immigrants stay. They follow seasons, crop after crop, hands green stained from cabbage leaves, backs bent potato-picking. Others before stuck it out. Airmen stayed and married Lincolnshire girls, building Polish or Ukrainian Clubs out of view, down side streets, scattered like seeds across even land. A little to the north a log-cabin scout hut is a Polish Roman Catholic church that used by airmen became rooted. Now, escapees from torture, or hankering for the motherland, keep filtering in, despite the signs, pinned to verges, knee-high, on B roads: 'No! To Asylum Seekers'. These contemporary residents have forgotten the generosity of the 'patron of the Fens', St Guthlac.

seasonal workers'
shed — who knows — rattling beside
a prairie of onions

Now on a metal road, Hospital Drove, some on the left verge, some on right. We needed our bottles of water. I tried to make my rucksack lighter shifting its position. Jo removed one top walking on in a tee-shirt, Barbara wore a laced blouse and my Toronto Maple Leaf's cap. She closed in, unzipped a pouch in my canvas sack, pulled a water-bottle for an extensive swig.

not really cirrocumulus
these spirits of the sky...
denim shirt-tails flapping

A youth hot-rodded past, no greeting or how-do-you-do, looking proud and 21st century-ish! Then turned around his black, four-wheel and zoom back! We gave him an inch more. I thought, 'listen I was turning corners on two wheels before you were born!' That was Canada. Then didn't drive for thirty years until, required for my job here. A few weeks ago I wrote off my car. I swerved to avoid an on-rushing red dart; it gouged, caving in the frame; a splinter from the mirror ricocheting off my glasses. When I kicked open the warped door, all I could think was the other guy OK. I, brought up in a pacifist mode, in a country that never commanded me to go off and kill, had come in inches of taking another human being's life.

I didn't think anyone on that walk guessed my inner darkness. I kept walking, sharing jokes. We examined a heavy-linked chain winding like a python from a house, and speculated what beast had been chained here and where was it now. The sound of growls and snappy barks leapt over a wall. Just kept eyes front, left/right, marched by. A farmer drove past in a coupé, his wife, I think, settled in the passenger's seat. He gave a quizzical look that said, only mad dogs and English men. A greeting, nothing chic, too civil, his salutation suggested us five, in the age of the car, were one of billions, part of the homo sapiens family.

poppies in a clump
make a roadside shrine
for the unknown motorist.

The day was about half gone. We had trekked three and a half miles. The sun had moved a degree from left of the road to right, reaching zenith and starting its luminous descent; its fire undiminished. Its bright arc copied the geodesic curve, but its unhindered movement, an illusion. It was our world that rotated in an orbit more rapidly than perceived. In keeping with that mis-truth, the five of us walked on the pre-Columbus earth toward a destination neither above, below nor behind, on the same level in front. A tractor, with global tyres rolled by, pulling a trailer. Inside the cab, a blue overalled driver was grumpy that a motorist had cut him off at the junction. We guessed where the cargo of feed was destined; a green field block-printed with chestnut cattle, unusual on our tour. When we reached the gated entrance, he had driven away. We watched cows with huge tongues lasso shafts of hay from bundles the farmer had broken and scattered. Near the gate our curiosity was drawn to a rusted implement. Its stiff conveyor-belt, like bony plates on a dinosaur visible above shrouding growth. A monster once chuffing and clanging! Now, grave-quiet, the old sorter disappeared into history calmly as it had vanished behind a screen of nettles and 'sticklebacks.'

rusted scars ditched in —
a field wreck
wrapped in bindweed
                    Barbara Elizabeth Harrison

We passed the aluminium outline of a canning factory, and another marker of time, invisible, except for a dotted line on a map. The Midland and Great Northern Railway stretched through these fields, a busy line in its heyday, the guide claimed, transporting goods and passengers. I pondered if summer children here, once knew by the evening mail-train's whistle that it was time to stop playing and go home, as Lincoln youngsters of a past era. A friend had told me, if your parents scolded you for being late in, you could never excuse yourself for failing to hear the London mail train's eight o'clock summons. It shook the city's back to backs. In her nineties, I recollected, my mum's recurrent tale from childhood — when her mum and dad (my grandparents) were early in Hamilton and settling in — she heard each night a lion roar from a nearby zoo, eerie in the darkness as if that lion was untamed and couldn't be ignored. The guidebook also noted, that the line had carried bombs from ammunition factories to Norfolk airfields. The echo of war speeding across a slow-paced geography. Brown-backed road signs pointed to this or that aviation museum and in church-yards from North Coates to Long Sutton resided commonwealth war-graves. Stones stood white and polished against less-cared-for greying monuments of locals who had grown from the soil returning to it, who over centuries never 'up sticks'. Commonwealth headstones marked the resting-places of new-comers, up-starts, interlopers, not foreign airmen who gave their lives in this nation's defence. I was an immigrant constantly in a state of displacement, like a conspicuous grave I couldn't blend into the surroundings, into the lichen-tinted desuetude. Someone would note my accent and say you're not from around here. I no longer received remarks as a curse, but a humble wink-and-a nod to my up-rooted-ness. In the far past, dislodgment had been necessary and people were forced to make new homes in Tons or small settlements connected by causeways, in some cases on islands reached by navigable vessels. From there fen sluggers would, embanking and draining, reclaim the land against fierce winds, long winters and flooding.

On the right we strolled by a strip of recent houses. Sally and I teased their newness and bravado; we were smug. I pointed out loopy lions and stretch-necked peacocks on the posts, guarding the entrance to one house after another. Homesteads had names like El Paso and Misty Glen. Such misnomers made a minor suburb, in the wide-open land, look stranger. But stood as a bastion too against the big field's mono-agricultural dominance. The assurance of exotic hollyhocks, scarlets, whites and pinks, wavered over garden walls, and along protected borders spread golden or yellow roses. Again, the group dispersed into pockets of dialogues. Looking back, I felt vaguely responsible, since I was leading this boot-camp length hike. But they looked content; I saw from a bag a notebook fly out to accept each penned observation.

The journey grew into a resistance to looking back, an endurance to carry-on, spliced with suspense and astonishment. Once more we bunched, as the flashing of vehicles on the A17 came closer, as we heard its tempered roar. Later, at a crossing point, no bridge or lights, we waited for a gap. In twos, except for Holly, we zipped across; Barbara and I holding hands.

Roads gave out. Ahead, beyond a wide gate, stretched a grassy bridleway, too wide for practical use of walkers or farm vehicles. A preserved old drove route that arable fields had not invaded, leaving this space to saunter through. A farmhouse planted by the way. Tall, small-brick walls held uncurtained sash windows, toward a shingled roof and sky-pointing chimneys, smokeless and still against the day's afternoon blue. We surveyed, inquiring if the property was inhabited. Through a groomed hedge a line of many-aged clothes rippled. Too distant from the structure; as if they must be someone else's garments, not the inhabitants, if there were residents, in that stand-alone building. Too reserved. Like the plumb, deeply-dug field-limits, even this house's front yard hadn't stolen an inch from the grass avenue. This perhaps virtuous non-aggression only increased the feeling that the house was unconnected to the present, a survivor, a remnant, allied to another age. Its windows looked so uncompromising. For a second, the broad way slipped from perspective into an endless corridor, abstracted from the landscape on either side.

bronze, green and yellow...
Rothko fields

Barbara Elizabeth Harrison

In graceful uniformity I sought shade by a boundary of hawthorns. Green berries foreshadowed autumn's cool reds. Shadow short-lived, the way unrolled, a wide carpet. I looked at my brown shoes dust-filmed. Before setting out, we'd debated about footwear. Sally decided on flip-flops, Holly sworn by her sandals; Barbara between boots and trainers, elected the latter as had Jo. Above cloud-shaped aspens, we made out angled arms of cranes on the docks at Sutton Bridge.

In our travel, we reached the point when bias of return outweighs forward momentum. We would bend back to the silver cone of St Mary's, seen far off. Our avenue tattered into heightened greens; a path swung to right, sloped to the shore of South Holland Main Drain.

perched on the bank
a paint-peeled signpost —
to the old and new world.

Before, with the water-route hidden, I was unsure how the word drain was being used. Below the lip of the agricultural plain, space pulsed with new intensity; we stepped into a trough, a frontier zone between embankments and mercurial slowness. Down at the edge, a released wind shivered leaf-pennants, thick tall reeds to a lion's roar. The ground speckled with dark blue flowers. I imagined, on the globe's other side, a nocturne of speckled stars. Mid-stream, my heart leaped. Sheltered from vistas; we reached a sanctuary, hugging the water's gleam, life hummed, flew, waded or manoeuvred. A mallard community startled by our appearance.

to the shore
descend — a skyline
at my right shoulder.

Our viewpoint what we saw and knew about a land's character. Nature had claimed back the drain cutting new fenlands. My reading told me: in an older topography, thousands had lived a thousand generations and had left a trace of their existence. I walked through environment formed from ideas of the 18th century Enlightenment. Straight waterways, fields squared to precise demarcation, roads formed into an urban grid; equal and rationalised space, as if the fens should look like the centre of Paris. Those builders created control and order if it meant illuminating dark marshes, straightening crooked ways; accepted evacuation of fen-sluggers. It meant progress. Fenners had possessed the land without ownership, lived, breed, trapped and made light of crooknecks, stilt-strided over unstable ground. They fought for two centuries, from Ancholme Carr to Cross Keys Marsh, to save their life-style, for another hundred years, before succumbing to windmills and steam-power. Finally they could fight no more. I fretted about what the poetic rebel against enclosure acts, John Clare, observed. Here, freeholders suffered doubly, end of common-land and advert of drainage restrictions. During the c. 19th. anti-fenlander propaganda critics were amazed that voices such as John Clare and Tennyson could be inspired to create poetry within these dark, dour, damp environments.

The dried, enriched land wasn't given back to original dwellers. It was sold, to pay for the engineering schemes; to outsiders who became gentlemen farmers, landowners. The poet Rilke says, every era leaves its dispossessed. Economics was not enough to enforce transformation. Were we five dispossessed — walking out there — at odds with the normal haste of reality? The past had to be vilified. Fensmen demonised as living 'in foule and woosie Marshe, supporters of chaos, enemies of organised life. They lived like Aborigines of North America,' a speaker of change raged, 'a kind of lawless life, almost in a state of nature, and their ideas, wild as their native Fens... not very easily subjected to reason or control'. Denouncements were made against the first nations of my continent and against Gaelic crofters — uncivilised, unworthy. Silence! My head! Silent the water passed without a wiggle of protest through the Enlightened landscape of Holland Drain. Not a vestige left. No Roman-styled ruins. No abbey remnants to shore up the parish church as at Crowland. For past fenners, museum bits in Spalding, duck-cannon, a punt, a few trinkets, legends of the Imprisoned Moon and Tiddy Mun. Cosmopolitan Macaulay maligned Fen Sludgers as 'half amphibious beings'. The fenlanders used everything that rose from earth and slipped below uncertain surfaces. They existed by, a now recognised, cyclic ecological creed. When the terrain was drained, their ways vanished. A genocide took place. Saintly outsiders became the isolated, deprived of decent customs, became by another twist, depraved, and by another worshippers of darkness lurking along sinuous routes. Their holy status reversed they were deemed in league with demons. Some saw the fen-people caught by delirious fancies of marsh fever who must be rescued. In the ninth century monks fled into the Fens to escape invaders and established outposts of piety and care for all living creatures.

dream-up — those
ancestral *sloggers* — hems
lapped by moonglow.

My companions re-captured my imagination. They complained about footless nettles, close to the ground, they got in above flip-flops to sting. Barbara and I shared our last water. The sun had moved an inch. The great percession had notched a millionth of an inch backward, not to where humanity stood, but to where it might stand thousands of years hence. The gleaming course placid, moved on, between grassy banks. Along the eastern edge, we gingerly made our way, slapping at horse flies, dodging nettles. Into the water wooden docks protruded, with number plates, where fishermen, with latest rods and tackle, competed for trophies.

between anglers
a huge dragonfly
retraces its empire

                                    with crested heads
                                    sword-shaped reeds
                                    clash on each side

off each cat's paw
the unhindered sun
keeps leaping ashore

                        disturbed
                     grey rags flap
                 heron's summer flight

                Barbara Elizabeth Harrison

Altered landscape bred mythologies. I could feel compassion
for engineers, planners with their fragile schemes to subjugate
nature's will. The struggle went on to keep water moving across
alluvium, to preserve fertile soil from wallowing inundations.
Many were drawn into the challenge, some whose family had
dwelt beside embankments for as long as anyone could remember;
others had been thrown into this contest to save the environment
through chance.

Prisoners of violence
bent and ached — shored up.
Stayed, planted roots.
Their children
stroll their laboured banks.

Members of present humankind, would dispute manipulation
was sensible, that draining dark morasses beneficial. I imagined,
to others, marshlands, wooded slopes, arable fields, pastures,
salterns were vital. Humanity engaged not to pierce gloomy
interiors of bogs and carrs, with reason's light; but to find
conducive skills to tend to each culture, preserving a balanced
ecology. Urges to conquer, colonise, exploit perceived as
misguided. 'Look at the golden-rod,' I shouted. 'Not golden-rod.

It's ragwort.' Sally corrected. The drain's bank offered many phenomena. Spikelets of grasses, honey-coloured, some sallow fading towards autumn, from midsummer, but stretching up like labial finials.

Call-notes, full, rapid. The group paused. Listened. Stared to glimpse the source of chittering. Then one, then another saw, adjusting sight to pick out camouflaged birds that clung to sedges or in skipping flights ascended to a dwarf tree. Barbara guided until I spotted small dull shapes. Then lost them in the rhythmic turmoil, behind the moving mosaic before our eyes.

reds almost daze,
a line of fireweed
on the opposite bank

Thirty summers ago I set out from Canada, a passenger on an ocean-liner, to see more of the world, escape the past. Hiked through this Island-land. From Tilbury docks, until I saw the Isle of Ely rise above surrounding fens, a Saxon foothold. I skirted Stamford, toward Nottingham, to white hills of Derby until north I reached where my grandfather had praise, the Lake District. I had returned to his country, lived here since; stood alone on the rising and falling bow, staring eastward, as he had stared west, imagining what the future would cast.

thirty-years ago
at the cutting edge
separating...life waves.

Holly told me of her collaboration with a friend, a proposed children's book with artwork and poetry. I could see the future in her eyes, aspiring but cautious, aware how things turn out different than planned. Hopeful. I stayed in England, after my oceanic trip. Seen something through. What would my grandparents think: disappointed that I had abandoned dreams of a better life or pleased that I had returned to their memory-filled birth-country? The drain's waterside teemed with insects; blue florescent damsel flies, singular or joined in a twosome. Bees worked the dotted flora. Sweating air full of wind and droning flies. Barbara, whose blood insects loved, had a minor bite on her left ankle. Jo and her sister conversed along the shore catwalk. Against polite rapport, a horse fly in hot pursuit causing Jo to bolt with little yelps. When we reached the bank's top, and saw in front and around fen horizons, a final confrontation occurred. The horse fly landed for a bite and received a fatal blow from Jo who swung her notebook. A white page left with a red smear. We were leaving that trough of nature. The track tilted up, moderating coolness of Holland Drain vanished against the sun-fire. Hitting level land, felt closer to the familiar world; sounds of traffic more pronounced. On the bank-top we saw rubbish left by midnight visitors who'd parked, I imagined, then, before love-making flung MacDonald's hamburger boxes and drink containers in a heap. Something would have to work hard to assimilate. We walked down Seagate, a little-travelled road that copied the line of the last outpost before sea-rages. Once, those tides withdrew, the whole world must have looked steadier, less hazardous to the first generation who conquered, with plough and spade, turned the loom-rich ground and on it built their homes.

Each walker made adjustments with their new-found-land. We turned from slow water and traits of ancientness. A minor rise, the group strode into an upper kingdom letting go of mid-journey fantasies, uncertainties; saw St Mary's tower beyond drapery of trees and houses: a sure landmark of arrival and conclusion. Our raised road divided history, the known and recordable on one side, the legendary untellable on the other. No coincidence known graves were 17th century; same age the first exertions to drain the fens partially succeeded. New-comers needed ground to inter their dead. Where, among morasses, oozy islands, did the earlier dwellers, Gyrvii, bury theirs? Place them in reed coracles, set on fire, set them adrift?

With that question lingering, our quest's end surprised. We climbed what no one would call a hill except where a humble knoll was valued as a rock outcrop against ubiquitous fens. We finished at the Library — our starting point. Arrived marching as if our tarrying related to desire to be endlessly observant. Now the illusion of energy-wasting heat passed away. The town in a haze, relieved no thunder shocks had broken out that hot afternoon, Long Sutton's roof tiles absorbing the light. It had returned to a self-effacing discreetness. The morning's excitement — the wedding party had dispersed, their escorting VWs garaged. We'd come full circle achieving a day; the fairy-tale sun lagged, had hours before it could repose so far to the west it would set in the north. Each participant hurried to pick up belongings, re-make connections, rides home, loved ones to inform. They deserted the adventure to re-enter the everyday that called us five to different beginnings. Each a stash, scribbles, perhaps a poem or two, kept secret or presented to a favourite reader. Never knew what became of those words hoarded that Long Sutton day. Three out of five of the co-wonderers I would never meet again.

afterwards
thirsting... for the bitter
quench of grapefruit
   Barbara Elizabeth Harrison

We May Never Heal Disappointment and Yet Find Love

The Diver

Perpendicular to the sheer cliff:
her caressing fingers ease around
pale ears, coax across the nape;
she guides and tucks her curls
until each haphazard glimmer's
hidden beneath her bathing-cap.
Streamlined, she flexes, raising
her heels and bracing spread toes,
springs from the bony platform —
four billion stars in a diver's arc
— almost a soundless entry —
stroke for stroke sets out to sea.

The Irregular Amputee

The therapist said
you should be a regular man
propel yourself with
strapped on artificial legs.

In the hospital clinic
beside a double-aspect window
one pointed to the street/ the other
towards an inner courtyard
of immense plastic forms
creatures that might creep
into your imagination
when between your long arms
you sway your body
like an infant on a swing
tease it back and forth,
spread palms bearing the earth,
over obstacles, a gravel path,
a fallen limb. Like an insect
you inch down the terrain's length.
Until you rest and gaze
and gaze, take in everything,
you tell me.

Urban Pastoral

Black poplars in a line: their taut leaves tapping
serenading like musical instruments as they might
when summer's past and autumn is yet immature.
You and I, candid, inside the shallow bus shelter,
no seats I recall; your grey coat was buttoned up
but who could misread your smile, that giggle?

Then I was going, against my plans, following
on to a coach with a spring your soft brown shoes
traveling from the city with squeezed in strangers
— you and I suddenly intimate, after one night.
I ignored spoken words, my promises to return.
You teased out a button letting my hand explore.
And yet I looked out the rounded window at us
passing and the row of poplars slipping behind.

The Fragile Man

The gentleman adored Edward FitzGerald's
translation of the Rubáiyát; he'd several editions.
It was his signature. He knew its Sultan's noose opening.

Some time ago, shaky, his left hand unwilling
to rest on the reading table, he gazed far off.
From a vase a troupe of purple hyacinths

perfumed the room; they smelt of the tulip lips
of desert girls. When Parkinson's overwhelmed, he let
his wife take a lover, allowed him into his home.

When caressing their way through passions
he didn't eavesdrop on their pillow-talk.
He was pleased no one called on his body.

In the Meadow

To A.E.

Fashion of clouds that late afternoon, puffed white sleeves
with trim of washed through blue; one bird had not lost
its liquid voice to drying sun and wind and across tops
of purple knapweed two brown butterflies doe-see-doed —
you might find love and never heal disappointment.

It wasn't the sterility in a parching southerly current
but our century's promoting of the mechanical above
the organic which muted bird songs, if at that moment
I couldn't hear the slug of traffic on the big nearby road —
we might never heal disappointment and yet find love.

The undersides of a snarled oak's grey-green foliage
glowed at times catching reflections off the slow water
that moved like rare beverage between aching grass
and I became a sinking leaf spinning in its stream —
you a snipped twig disappearing into the next meander.

Married Life:
A Sufi's Quest

Cyprus, New Morning

Giant pink-orange
rising, stirs the orchard
with winter colours

white valley houses
catch. Somewhere lorries
growl at an ascent

warming beams
stripe the grove — a palm
waves its welcome.

Marriage Suite in North Cyprus

1. Near Girne
(before our marriage)

Our escort's red beetle
gets a flat — we peel
& eat three oranges
picked from the ground.

Blue, dark slate, turquoise
roll in and break throwing
manes of white against
Crusader Castle walls —
honeycombed to coral.

building sites around
grimy olive groves — new houses
creep up the sacred slope.

Jinn's mountainface unmoved
two whole days we've been
among Girne's dust

2. After our wedding day

Purring pines go quiet
all night rain trickles
for spring in two weeks

silent smoke
circles evergreens
till under a spell

uncrackling
mist weaves
up Komando tepe

dripping — a shower —
night rounds the grapefruit
in a guest house garden

Sofina's oval face
in fireglow — like the moon
before it was moon.

3. *Above Girne*

St. Hilarion —
a white-tuft robin watches
by ancient monk's cell

we climb the cloudy
stair-path — against advice
of those descending

a minute in view
the sinking sun enflames
Besparmak peaks

4. *After staying in a motel rotten with fleas*
For Sofina

You kiss me and —
Mediterranean foams ashore
with love in its heart.

You sing — swirling
turquoise waves — a kind siren
who won't shipwreck me!

5. At Cyprus' end of the world

Zafer Burnu —
two shorelines touch
a high marker groans.

two sounds & tempos
undermine cliff-rocks
north and south.

timid flashing eyes
a wild donkey glances out
through thorny climbers

from the cape
islands broken away
dwindle to surf

The Mosque of Seven Companions

built on low rocky seashore —
when Greek Cypriots dominated the area
was reduced to a household residence; now stands
restored to a maqam or sacred site.

Inside Hazrat Ömar Mosque, you —
twenty-five years a covered Muslim
and I — five days from my Shahada —
submit before the tall green alcove
its unfigured hollow topped with
calligraphy you wish you could read.

The Mediterranean's cadences
sound through beats of thought.
Breakers could snarl and hurl
storm-froth on the shelter's roof
yet no weather-mood can perturb
seven green turbaned saints inside.

When, from eight centuries of warring
empires, Ottoman foot soldiers ducked
into a cave and chanced on, laid-out,
unaged bodies of seven companions
they appeared no more than children
cuddling for warmth, ready to awake.

The mosque's far-eyed attendant
collects for the abstract-bordered
sajada we buy. Then, off duty,
discretely steps out and taking a rod
casts for what he might discover
in rolling turquoise brightness.

In darkness, I see unknown mountains,
enveloped with evergreens, curl
toward seven bare-stone summits
each wrapped in unwarpable
brilliance. You, standing closeby,
recite Arabic — *Ya Siin.*

Slow that cosmic prayer moulds
the shore-rocks of our grief and love.

No Trains in Cyprus

Like two comets through
the Muslim North's pre-dawn
sit tight behind high beams
from Ömar's on-call minibus
as prayer beads swing
from his rear-view mirror.

Unruffled by its rocky shore
the Mediterranean's moon-beady.
Asleep Besparmak's headstones
with red valleys crimson as the up-
yawning sun. Skirting Lefkosha,
on the dual carriageway's verge
day-work gangs wait for transport
huddle like surrendered soldiers.

Be in good heart at departures;
walk straight on to the runway
at Erçan; climb steel stairs to join
the flight; ignore stern-browed
passengers who think you're late.

After crossing the mellow eastern Med
observe through your lidless porthole
Anatolian heights polished with snow.
The airline tips and a coastal plain flows
into view with giant palms like windmills.

Over morning Istanbul, far out of hearing
of the Blue Mosque Adhan, nibble wrinkly
stowed dates, the best, sticky Iranian. Then
bury respectfully each sucked-dry stone
in the seat-arm's obsolete fag-snuffer.

Take brief looks like sips of water
through gaps in cloud-oceans below
as the twin engines' magnetic purr
pulls lovers and strangers homeward.

For an age be conked out.

Today the North Sea's dozy
— short white tails of trawlers
fizzing along a crepe tissue plain.
Then curves of the English coast
level as a folded out chart, as if
nothing could hold the water back.
Until the airline's shadow grows
over the chimera below. The cabin
de-compresses and a child screams.
Turkish wheels skid on British terrain.

Board early; catch the Robin Hood Line
through green-ness familiar with hedges,
fences, passive partitions where a horse
lowers its chestnut head, a gardener digs
by fairy-lit bushes and white seed puffs:
— all far from war-zones. On the fens,
so primed for flight, assembled swans
all at once hesitate. Afternoon passes.

The train makes good time through
Cambridge to Ely. At Peterborough,
more journeyers press to snatch up
an empty seat, two, one for luggage.
Before any step off a lunging army
scuffles to invade. Push and Shove.
Be brave. Take it in stride, as when
you were once regaled as a foreigner.

Squeezed into a single unit, all the way
to Spalding; later stay strum, among
vacant seats, when a line-switch jolts.

But ignore all this. Gaze into escaping day
and recall dawn's remote land. Recall
its ancient towers, church bells silenced
strapped-in by iron bars, its roads booming
from canvas-backed trucks, crammed with
teenage recruits, its crisp red flags flapping.
Keep a weather-eye on lingering twilight
mat-ceilinged with brushed over orange
just above a gentle, Güzelyurt Bay blue.
Reflect how the cost of peace is so high.

'A Cure for Hay Fever'

On the warped board, you clutch a Cyprus
grapefruit in your hands, rub its cheeks

not yet wanting to taste this blessed
gift from a Shaykh, its tropical scent.

Deep or thin covered, your thumb
stroking its gold-yellow pitted skin

you refuse to plunge inside. Let it
remain a rescued ornament, moon-shone,

surface cratered, a lissom Scarface.
You imagine attacks it endured

in a walled, exile's garden, quaking
with others on the same ropey

branches. Hurricane-flailed, it kept
its outward crust, never fell and burst.

You idle, longing to know: whose grip
brought it down before reaching yours?

Visiting Eyüp Sultan

Under bow, fish in sun-purged
schools and jellyfish, our ferry
planes the morning Golden Horn,
our wake like glittering shavings —
with Ayasofia on the left hill.

You and I, disembarking, join
noon wayfarers through an arch
in a mosque precinct wall, stutter-
stepping in a crush at Eyüp Sultan.

We pray on unrolled street-size carpets.
Three tall plane trees bellow shade
and for one, five centuries old
an elegant grille's wrought iron
has imprinted its immense bole.

Inside, blue geometric tiles
border an alcove's silver tomb
I feel the stopper being pulled
from an unnameable
fragrance. Infirm worshippers
slide smooth or craggy hands
into a shiny footprint's well
and lather their faces.

I believe what I see
a hairpin's pearl-tear
on a pale colour hijab
seeks intercession.

Outside, an ice cream vendor
with an entertainer's chuckle
rattles his long stick in his tub

and like a magician teases
our each attempt to buy.

Wind-bowed, far aloft,
we enquire of each other —
two festive kites, over the mêlée —
who possibly directs them?

In quick response
a youngster lifts a gold sceptre
(disbelief tinging his cheeks)
dressed-up a little sovereign
in his circumcision robes.

We treat our slumped stomachs
with corn on the cob, charcoaled.

Our teeth more than treacled
soon we stand and wait for the return ferry;
grey swells against black buffing tyres.

A knowing boatman carves
his curved approach, digging in his oars
he rows fresh visitors along shore:
his passengers lounge side by side,
tanned forearms and showy hairstyles,
adolescent couples on a Sunday outing.

Out in the broad, punchy Bosporus
crossing the worldly shipping lanes
we're motioned off the foredeck
(too easy to be washed overboard).

We arrive, our prow thumping
a gnawed late afternoon dock.
Untraditionally touching
you stagger back into me.
Minarets of Usküdar loop the sun.

Peace Be Upon Him

You prayed, alone, in a mountain hole
through shrill night. No voice responded.
I pray in darkness in my walled-in heart
among ageing ambitions' heaped junk.
You knew unending illiteracy of being
and struggled through doubts, delusions,
before the Angel spoke; before converts
and fleeing for your life; the miraculous...
you lowered your covered head into rock
centuries had swirled and howled to sand.
Your daughter time to time brought food;
some Mekkan dates with well water I imagine.
You bowed not knowing light would come;
submitted against fear's rush. What beasts
might emerge? With lit eyes they perhaps
watched, waiting to see if you'd retreat.
In an absent room, my prayer mat glows
a rectangle of sanity; on knees I shake
repeating salawats; through my fingers
a tasbih rattles. From inside, faces gawk,
hornless devils or angels. More than past
your presence: is my quaking your doing?
You prayed bookless, no script written, your
knees imprinting glints. Before the mission
announced or you were entitled Messenger,
you felt emptiness; heard claims of lunacy —
everyone's distracting alarm; but yet went
on in worship before the Angel at last spoke
Read. 'I can't read' your humble words back.
When you slid down the scree and later told
Waraqah your vision, you looked in disbelief
that you would need to arm yourself with God.

Sayyida Aisha Disobeying?

The Prophet (peace be upon him) had been instructed by Allah the Sublime to leave his sleeping wife's lap and go and stand among, and pray for, the dead in Medina's necropolis in the middle of night. Certainty of direction. Imagine the Messenger's sandaled feet pressing into the silted earth as his arms were raised in supplication, in Du'a. His high turban's green tail ruffled on his neck as his voice thrilled the deep sleepers. His human weakness called on to uphold the weight of the newly and distantly departed; to intercede for them, a finite being counter-balancing the infinite. Did he intercede, call for each separately remembering an excellent action from their lives, a reason for pity, present them as individuals to Allah? Or did he sweep the deceased into his heart's arms, ask for their forgiveness as a community to his Lord? His feet aligned with the Ka'ba, it seemed a human figure was the pole around which worlds rotated. Sweat glistened like stars on his face. His wife Aisha followed. Her curiosity stirred night clothes, she stalked her man. She longed to share in the incredible mystery as much as she could. It had touched her when the Prophet lifted his head from her pillowing thigh when Allah Almighty summoned. Did she hear an echo or vibration of that Calling? What had touched her in that sudden vacuum as her beloved slipped into the night; what pulled her to stand back for the duration, a watcher? She must have her role, in the vast act of praying for the dead, since her young womanhood had been caressed by Allah's Beloved. She knew she had a right to follow, risk disobeying, to show her love could breathe near that other love. Such moments she would stow for her seclusion after the Prophet's (pbuh) death. That night her feet orientated towards God's House in Sunna. She recorded the event passing on to us its wonder. May Allah Most High be pleased with her.

To My Wife

I know that we humans won't
always be here to observe the slow
colour-change around still water,
won't be to let our cheeks brush
against a bulrush's seed comb,
with pinging ears listen to chimes
from a reed's finery or at our feet
see into the heart of wildflowers.

You bend, no longer young, then
crouch down among their colours
scattered across the sibilant land
as a faint pattern on a dancing dress,
right down till you half-disappear
into wasting green. Your pilgrim

scarf — not protecting your hair —
but down around your waist, tied
as a teenager might an excess layer.
When you reach, pick and gather
I sometimes take-in the suffering
that twinges through your each limb.

Those final generations mightn't
be so naïve, caught-off guard when
theirs and our world shuts down.
They will see how consciousness
that fragile alert thing is handed on.
Far off they'll hear its new carriers,
gauge their arriving like muted steps
to a broken gate. When light streams
down the coldest hill they'll fade and
know the flower's heart will be seen.

Swans on Kielder Water

Ochre boundaries dip. Under greenest larch,
on the water, trumpeting white adults glide,
with heads raised, unseen, giant paddling webs
manoeuvre. In an in-let they crowd and idle
obscured except for their chatter, their beaks'
sounding horns above first light's reflection.

Many, so many know this secret rendezvous
— where to dive from the sky, where to angle
earthward, to gather. Alert to invading steps,
half the company shrills alarm. They lift wings
to flap and flap as if against the solid water's pull
nothing could ascend. Yet snake necks straighten
to a flight of spears; wing tips slap with aching beat
till water gives and warning creatures rise to touch
-down in a more remote bay to speak their wisdom.

Thunder Afternoon
during Ramadan

to honour my wife who took a
vow of silence as part of her fast

You won't eat — to rest
and cleanse the stomach, or talk
to soothe, clean your tongue.

You let the phone blare —
you put your hand on your heart
and I turn speechless

like a sounding box
every passing sound vibrates
in your day's silence.

Now, in loud meadow
far beyond the cricket grounds
by a wisping Rase

a queen settles on
her cushioned throne — a bee lands
on purple knapweed

I make quick wudu
catching first drops from deluge
in cupped crinkled hands

the cooling storm swirls
like arrows in a vortex
thin sun-blond grasses

fast from onyx ranks —
topaz, ruby, beryl — a half
rainbow gems the east

for your afternoon
swifts, pulsing and screeching,
abstain from our sky

between thunder-shocks
my dripping shifty shadow
is a missing friend.

My heart takes the vow
to listen more. Mallards swim
pleased their path's refreshed.

I pick goose-weed burrs
off my clothes — then lift the latch
to your calm garden.

So much sorrow dis-
appears, without a comeback
in our un-telling.

Apples

for Afifa

Before making a crumble
my love whittles out the bad,
peels and places small apple
boats in a bowl of water

Spires and
Minarets

Some years ago I walked through Lincolnshire fens and heath between Lincoln and Sleaford to the south. I recorded impressions in poems and prose — the landscapes and communities I passed through in May when hawthorn and campion were in bloom. I had already converted to Islam, becoming a Sufi Muslim three years before.

A Campion's Blush

across a lagoon
of young wheat — an island-wood
you'd need wings to reach

I won't walk this route
alone — so many will share
who've never been here

my first wife steps out.
once I dreamt to spend midnight
with her in such a green-surrounded wood

clay ground dry and split —
even few rainy sun-drops
welcomed on a leaf's face.

The Find

After the striding jacketed woman
with two roughly same aged children
passed by with a dog they called Hector,
on the thin bridleway, I knelt down
to a clue: a narrow plastic hair-band
with some Milky Way's shimmer
along it between naff love hearts.
I picked it up, combing my finger
on twin inside ridges of tiny teeth.
Then threw it away into green cover
among dense currents of bluebells
thinking that a better resting-place.
But the pinkish arc shone back in
a sun-shot between trees, beckoning;
I had to retrieve and pocket the thing.
Till stepping out of the wood's shade
at the young wheat's loud edge, at once
I thought, I should've left it on the path.

At Digby Church

dedicated to Thomas à Becket

> Twelfth century arch
> a bird's artful weaving
> above carved chevrons.

At Digby, Evening

After spring's long aridness, late afternoon cloud came in gangs.
The sky thumped with long downpours. Then a rainbow branded
the eastern escape routes. I stroll around the churchyard; looking
up, find finial-clustered spires at each broach of the steeple,
each further probing into the sky. Inside, I read the list of 1604
plague victims; determined to go down all the names, status, first
names and family members. My eyes leap from the photograph's
original record, damaged and in an alien cipher, to the modern
transcript. They're side by side on the west wall in the same slim
frame. Against one list's clear type imposes the other — a stained
river's wild scribbles. I keep trying to make connections between
different names, puzzling if they were, or how they might be,
related. Somehow making links reduces, in my mind, each sufferer's
individual anguish; makes my reading tolerable. To be a
community meant something, especially in disaster, it hinted at
love. I imagine the rotation of mourners. Then, I withdraw. Finding
more secure ground outside, gaze at the tower's stonework,
guessing where Saxon centuries concluded, then where the
Norman, the Early English, and then ours began. I continue around
through wet illuminated grass, twice, then back to the west frontage.
Finally I pause, intrigued enough to investigate a relatively recent
bench in a small enclave — a childlike place — with a low hedge-
row surrounding it pointing in an eastward direction. With the
back of my fingers I rub the rain-haze off an engraved plaque. This
wooden seat is dedicated to a Canadian, born in Digby, who after
many years living ten thousand miles away, was flown back home

to be buried here. Drifting round the site, I ruminate on where my own resting-place will be, in my homeland Canada or my home Britain. Lincolnshire's unbounded sky discloses far curtains of rain that run and waver under cumulus in fleets obscuring the blue beyond. For a second, the approaching squalls look like ephemeral tornadoes. Two woodpigeons stay motionless on power lines, suspended in mid-air as if they don't need wings to elevate. That village son returned from everything he once must have enjoyed, discovered and marvelled at: the Rocky Mountains, the Pacific's curved horizon and sky-scraping redwoods. But he wished to come back to lesser heights, to the more modest landscape of the fens and perhaps his plague ancestors. Before I left on this walking tour, my kind wife said, I hope you always find a different route to journey along. She doesn't like taking the same path back from anywhere. There are so many returns, u-turns and back-words, that it's often hard to know which is the way forward.

> On his moulded bench
> massive raindrops — or I'd sit
> try to share his vista.

Next Day

> At Walcott I find
> a bus shelter where I can
> sit and scribble down.

> On the fens, overhead, an ocean.
> Ahead it's a jagged blue sliver
> in the distance; hard at my heels
> rain's marching nail-studs until
> a corncrake announces the next
> short clearing: was that white flash
> a hawthorn petal or scented hailstone?

soaked on the northwest
side from head to foot
like a tree carrying moss
I stroll into Walcott.

profuse daisy-chains —
is a field always sacred
near Catley Abbey?

Find II: Nothing to lift, retrieve or pocket

Catley Abbey doesn't exist. Yet this morning my B & B landlady told me her son-in-law cared for the site. I walk to Walcott, nearest village, search for inferences of the sacred, deliberating if nearby where the terrain slowly slopes up if the abbey once stood there. Grange Street, on a low sign, seems another clue. Tall grasses, moisture-and-sun turned, shine. Where is this non-existent abbey? And still it doesn't seem that strange, but exactly human, to care for something that no longer exists… but is too deeply written into emptiness to be discarded just like the corncrake or skylark tooling space with sharp metal song. I have to imagine the sculptor's mallet and chisel digging chevrons and worshipful forms into ashlar and sandstone: a monk below instructing. On island-mounds hardly above engulfing marshy fens, hermits and mendicants founded outposts. Perhaps Catley attracts 'special attention' because of the holiness, if inconspicuous, that's interred below its coarsened green surface. But what's protected and how's care shown: the grass cut, wind-scourged debris raked up and removed, that somebody knows the pigments on vanished statues and can report that a famous screen was buried, resurrected and later used in a nearby parish church? Someone takes time to observe, (doesn't listen to spectral choirs) but inhales May-scented boundaries, comprehending the monastic divide that runs across varied tones of age and olive green. Does any of this insist on a carer? No walls to maintain or children to warn off; nothing to charge for; a non-memorial, not a thing to cast a sun-dial's shadow.

Unlike ruins at renowned Rievaulx, Catley has no skeleton-shapes to try to deny the historical facts of wreckage and likely carnage. At that prominent site so much remains to defy an era's close. There the spirit appears to idle, waiting until another corps of stones is rebuilt; stands erect, colourful and powerful when our land's faith's restored. At Catley a few monks vainly repelled Henry's dissolution troopers (though Cromwell's blamed for scrubbing the reds and golds off the stone angels). Here no grey vestiges rise to mock resistant sainthood, or ruse of form exists to deceive imagination into thinking that the spirit doesn't migrate to new worlds, new expressions, new beliefs, but stays forever in its tenth century field: an instance — perfecting nostalgia. Catley makes little pretence to the eternity of place. What remains to be tended, is just an absence. Its imaginary edges can be soothed and swabbed, even nursed by caring hands. But in a mad rush, it seems, Catley's essence, its reality fled from the site. And yet, the abbey couldn't help but leave — in that wrench — a wound of love in the fen's side.

> Shelter by whitest flowers
> and partly open ash greens,
> from a farmyard's concrete
> watch a passing deluge dive
> into blackest loam speckled
> in rows with urgent growth.

> *Between fierce showers*
> *At Zuhr, where Catley Abbey once stood*

> Beautiful, God creates, makes
> and shapes the entire universe
> endlessly: each sky and pond
> every span of cushioning grass.

I celebrate His water, limpid
among reeds & first flowers,
I can scoop up for my ablution.
Honour His blue sky stretching
hidden lungs with aerial blasts
till I'm so eager to praise Him
with voice. I salute the grass
that allows me to spread out
this prayer rug, surrendering
under my full prostrate weight.
Sublime, God planted the pond
as if water had searching roots.
Carved cloud like fancy stones
to raise them to dizzy structure.
The Subtle, He rolled out grassy
fields as His own scented carpet.
Look to Him, The Magnificent.
the Beloved of all the Worlds.

Find III: Catley Abbey, This Nothing

Under a tubular gate to the next field
after rain, stubborn clay is still cracked.
To the south-east, a remnant pond glints.
I hook saturated satchel and dripping cape
on a maytree's shorn staff, asking: is it
alright for my belongings to hang here?
Then stumble down to an elusive edge.
The pond swallows drops then dilates
with acres of ordered sky mirrored in
unplumbable depths. I climb back up.
Round the vague site, fawn hares leap,
dash through obedient grass and clover;
white flecks disappear to moulded earth.
A pheasant wings it, barking its warning

over greasy turf crossed by bumpy ridges;
in troughs, marsh spikes trace lost conduits.
Not an object protrudes above hummocks,
all's settled below: sliced off angelic wings
old legends of miles-long escape-passages,
promises from Gilbertine monks and nuns.
A few wildflowers wave, spotted through
uncut growth. No residing loam descent.
At the double gate, it takes all my power
to loop over their posts — two blue ropes.
Exhausted, I'm blown into open space;
level to each magnetic point, the green
pulls far away from a modest ascent,
a sacred island of nothing, maybe.

Another Day

Find VI: Playing Environment

A lyre, a cello, a horizontal guitar
I strum three new lines of barbed wire
candidly taut between nail-gunned posts.
My thumb presses; plucks a grey glimmer
and releases each strand to make a bowless
solo thrum that carries no distance. I survey
the crude fence meant to stop each passing;
test tension and pitch down its bare length.
Without my touch, a west wind transforms
gnarled deciduous to sound with a whining
sparse-leafed insistence. A whipping gust
wins no rhythm or note from strung barbs
that need my fingers' pulse. In fallow land
some forgotten year's residual grain stalks
'sussle' and rustle; an earlier season's crop
surviving broad beans join the ensemble.

Three power lines, T pole to T pole stretch
following the path's corrugations and I listen
but their accompaniment's beyond hearing.
Then circuiting jets, from above the clouds,
send down their own sharp recoils, tunnel
passages, groaning and thundering, twist
tightening bands of unseen barbed wire.

In the Garden at Digby Manor

Violet-bluish horns —
ground ivy rounds a moss-robed
sculptured female nude

What's human time but
expecting death… on the way
abandoned to life?

Yellow can't unfurl
in this wind. Vast blue patches
at once filmed with white.

Stone venus puzzles
why she should stand here: left hand
asleep on her breast?

Among many more
a golden duckling crosses
the seed-freckled pond.

Down among tall flags
for a time the day remains
a straw nest of light

I wish Love's griever
could see — loving little things
helps heal the whole world

she demurs, half smiles
through eye-slits downward dreaming,
left knee faintly flexed

at peace but perplexed
why her small heart must carry
much more than she knows.

* * *

Love-scented hawthorn
Rowston's slenderest steeple
over chestnut blooms.

Visiting St Clements, Rowston

Find V: Grief

A key-holding woman with short grey hair, in black sweater and slacks opens the ancient interior. She directs me to a tympanum behind a wooden screen; draws my eyes toward a swirling pattern adzed in stone. Its interlacing lines, cruciform grooves with rounded edges convolute in organic manner. Four equal currents flow in a fluid knot, each weaving out through the centre to the limit then turning back towards the heart once more. My guide says, as a child she had, endlessly, drawn this pattern — an obscure symbol of complete inclusive unity. I imagine her innocence giving voice to silent stone.

Yours, my friend, that modern sculpture in Dorrington, you carved in wood unknown persons trying to hold up an undefined object. The object's circular as the huge bole of the tree that once stood and fanned its limbs. Then only the trunk survived and you carved into it. Do your figures support our sky? Feel fear of insignificance that weighs on villages: corollary of protected seclusion? Those straining faces look discontent as they struggle. Your work has no title or plaque like the carvings on the tympanum.

Its symbol resonated to worshippers, as still, now, the celebrated, Tudor-scripted panels of Ten Commandments resound, a little dustily, through the church. My escort — when a youngster — with thin-wristed hand, inscribed not that obvious spectacle from her village religion, but a redundant, secretive form. Her action's a plucked fact, like my knowing you are the author, chisels in hand, of the humanity in relief at Dorrington.

She left the church a while ago with the simple phrase, 'Stay as long as you wish. Just shut the door when you leave and it will lock itself.' Alone in this tomb and birthplace, a rampant blackbird, a power mower and the wind, force entry. The Knights Templar used this church: their order's fate, another sorrow of history. How can that injustice be redressed? St Clement, a martyr too: an even hazier figure, going back further in time. Here, each overt reality is supported by less definite existence; more misted, by less verified evidence. Insubstantials hold up this listed building's presence, its architecture and congregation. I marvel again how one of its members discovered perhaps, after Sunday School, in a moment alone, the strangest design on the most archaic stone and copied it down. Then had to do it over and over; it could never be complete, deserted. Sometimes, the least understood image, or hardly noticed silence, breaks the surface of the everyday; demands unbroken attention. Nearer bond, the more recognised work, fades into background. The here and now slips away almost forgotten.

I think that's how grief takes us: that supreme sorrow that strikes at love's defeat, before it's had a chance to play out a future. That distress, perhaps, only the young know and only know once, arises to dominate the present. Such suffering seems when encountered — impossible to comprehend. Where does it come from? From one heart or all hearts passing through one that weeps and screams? Between flashes of sense, the inflicted organ cries 'Why me?' I've thought ritual answers that out-burst, if incompletely. Ritual is an act in which reason appears to falter as everyday logic does under the pressure of acute grief. Like scribbled pages, sacred ceremonies are over written until illegible; exist as performances beyond practical need. Some retained elements, like the convoluting stone pattern, surpass meaning, yet pull us towards observation, repetition and awe. Grief, too, demands. The gravest grievers can't repel. They sink below the present and causality into the sub-territory of The Templars, tympanum and the unknown; sink beyond natural justice and tenable remedy, and sometimes won't surface for years.

A stone face stares. No recognition in that visage; grieving's concealed. Is a face needed? In an interior absent of effigies, images or figures would meaning be more graspable, tactile? I have seen where no grotesque glares from facades, high walls paved with beautiful serene calligraphy. Yet an unfathomable grief breathed in that script.

Last night, somewhere else, I met the severe mourner who in each direction saw her forfeit. All acts or routes lead back to the core of pain. She was youthful and could look — not outstanding or archetypal — but beautiful if desired. She had been a common-sense person; then through loss, that status as the excessive complainant, she's become a deity that can't be comforted. The transition shocks her as much as her grief. She's early in bereavement, some might say, and still in love with the one who's vanished. Yet, there is no end or measure to her agony; terms such as early, late or big or small are obsolete. It fills every object, household or artistic, loads each second and occupies her sleep.

Elegant structures with iconic or un-pictorial splendour must've been built in part for her. Each ashlar haunted expression, inexplicable angel and their rituals were designed to serve, to bring her through death to new life, to guide her from tomb to the birthplace. She thinks there's nothing out there for her. It hasn't been written and no one who hasn't 'lived' her grief could or would write about it. Last night, she spoke and each around the table saw an earlier imprint of themselves. I did, and disputed if my anguish had been once as colossal as hers. Every journey leads to finding or re-discovering grief. Viewpoints, such as seeing sorrowing like a journey, are meaningless. She sees no trip to or away from, but believes she carries it all right now. No human perspective will do. That's why she looks to need portals and stone guises to humanise her; must have this cold shell without praising voices, stark drooped slits of despair on the wall or the alarming word un-imaged. Often, the mourner needs the recurrent action that's beyond sensible, needs convoluted ingenuity of a pure shape like calligraphy or that a child parishioner crayoned — ancient carving that speaks and says nothing. What voice is that: of abstract motif whose meaning has vanished, yet calls us to attend again and again? Not lost to the final despairer who might find in that indecipherable blank a glint, a nick of light. Last night I learned again that we can rarely soothe the discomforted with words or perception; but must try to find tricks, sleights of hand, devices, artful or ingénue, to escort her to the form or ritual that could comfort but remains beyond knowing.

It's past the time — by politeness and respect for the old lady's and village custom — I should've departed. This House will stay peerless and quizzical after I close the door and step into May brightness. Each carving, direct and unashamedly obtuse, will hold back substance. The wind beats. Stray draughts snake between pews and through stone space where a group of the disgraced Knights once prayed toward Jerusalem. Over the way, in the west wall alcove, above where tea and coffee are served after the service, glimmers the oldest glass roundel. Possibly too fragile for a volunteer to tidy and polish until it looks glossy as adverts announcing the church's world purpose. The deep round opening is left untouched as if an alien place, as if a wound that can't be tended.

wispy cobwebs
swaddle surviving glass —
none can see through.

Last Day

A scented grotto
the sticky path's white-petalled
to a mare's paddock.

I journey between spires. The sun's infrequent; field tracks wet
and puddled, creviced earth slippery; trouser cuffs muddy
and often drenched or 'wetchered' some in these parts say. The
air's warm, insect-swarming. Spit out two I near swallowed.
Martins zoom to ground level, scoop over hedgerows. Cumulus,
like antediluvian cities crowded with floral terraces, pass by
wedged between grey plains; this immediate sky reveals all
weathers of time. The wind drops, the way broadens to a part
gravel, rutted track. I pass sheared sheep against graphic green,
under an estate's wall. Copper beeches rise in scarlet purple, sun
glows, cloud shadows. I come to another crown of spires. Blankney
drifts in and out of view.

simple butterfly
leaps the restricted byway
cloaked in burning white

Time to time reveries take me. I happen on a statue, half
sheltered under a tree-hedge. No joint effort busy with many
hands, as at Dorrington. A six-foot king tries to lift from earth a
stone, with raw, gripping fingers. The sword has been removed or
not yet stuck into solid rock. He appears un-chosen, a near-misser,
struggling with fate. His gaze laboured but open, welcoming, taking in
passers-by without sympathy or reproach. He doesn't stake a claim.

He's engaged in his task. Seats-stumps provided for the traveller to rest and see if the king can budge the obstacle. I can't stay. Walk on; his right eye follows, a clear pupil. Return for a longer look. His head out of alignment with his neck, a disablement that makes him look inflexible. But his torso is vast; extending arms stretch far down to the crude block. His hands determined, fingernails scratch new runes on its surface. My gaze is pulled to his enormous chest with subdued breasts, I see, from their bark cover, a warrior woman burst out with raised sword, from the splitting trunk.

I leave the king and queen. Follow signs, when sparse celebrate freedom and uncertainty; resist fears of never arriving, walking in circles. Then too many arrows. Choice is disquieting and the supplied map not helpful. Between villages, arrival is inevitable. At times I suspend disbelief. A plover calls, dips up and down, screeches, swoops; battles air, with awkward wings that look too big, all existence. It finds passages to advance over fine harrowed fields, ready to crash land. Unlike the blackbird, singing from a yard-perch, more like a curlew crying glides across moor. The plover hardly allows a glide, is boxing with space, grappling for height.

I stare, sweating from cloud's blue impact, shocked by the unlocked beauty. I imagine God as mad, beyond measure or logic and Creation His act of greatest unreason. God created nothing from sober reflection among barrenness, or for his instant pleasure. Conception was God at the most sacred extreme. Couldn't contain His Love. It flooded from Him, a spurge of indecent beauty, nothing controlled, a rush of scent, sound, smell, taste and sense that produced beings in their millions. A super-numerous existence. Sometimes, my loving wife says, think how much more there used to be: profusion of animals, plants, micro-creatures and uncountable life-forms. Nothing reasonable or orderly in that first explosion — Infinity's life-bang! From God's mouth Love flowed. His speech — with lunacy and uncomputable numbers — creation was perfect. I stroll through terrain's monocultural agriculture, un-hedged fields with the same crop. Estranged corners, chaotic ditches, a grotto of hawthorns or a stream's sloping sides break monotony. Fallow land hints at lost exuberance. Remnants from the crazy God's amoré survives like a shadow of a beard across farm fields. The mystic, following a divine way, is thought insane; his vast praise, disorderly; his desire for annihilation, suicidal. That servant longs to be swamped in a procreative surge as if God could re-make it again: Creation a repetitive art. Can existence's delta-bursting wave come again? For the devoted it can; countless extinct creatures revived. I pass a wood's edge; the trees lean across the bridleway, rattle overhead. Think on unnumbered living things. In the past, when travellers were robbed and stabbed, left for dead by the way side, they expired in that million millions of life. Their blood drained into grass and weed's micro hinterland, but they knew the universe was beyond control, and beautiful. Died in infinitude's lap. Over-populace was redemptive, unconstrained order, a blessing. Those destined for heaven, and others for Hell, walked through the same paradisiacal profusion: the countless songs and illimitable scents, almost sainted before raised up or swallowed. Now, we humans appear to wreck creation; our desire to manage, stifling multitudes, shrinking nature until patches of outrageous vegetation remain. We die in control's sterility, in our clinical washed-out colours. It's as if humankind, the height of creation, bites God's toes, pinches His side. So little we regard ecology and natural surroundings — His generous out-pouring — we slap His face, smash a glass bottle over the Eternal's head; disparage His beauty. God retains His madness until the end. He doesn't take stock, won't sober up and act reasonably, prepared to defend what's His, like a householder catching a burglar. God cherishes creation too much, with a love that defies understanding, like someone besotted; we are His created, fields stamped with our dictates, not just fences or barriers, but the entire pattern. His anger's withheld, His absurd mercy overwhelms sense. He delays. He delayed bringing life into being, He postpones its destruction. Seeing this pure un-reason, proud earth-wreckers think God dozes, doesn't exist or doesn't care as if creation was a fling, something abandoned to our managing hands. But God, That One, continues. He won't respond till His time, but waits, so teaming with affection for His creation, that it appears He loves what he hates; forgives what He forbids. The mystic, Sufi or saint knows to mirror this strangeness, to bless his enemies, to love what opposes him, what could cause him pain and loss, his stealth-killer approaching, or another that lurks in ambush.

I sit in the porch of St Oswald's at Blankney, behind a screen door to keep birds from building nests over the archivolt. The church is closed. A woman in high wellies with two dogs marches by, angling across the graveless lawn. A young man comes to the south side and peers up at the tower and its scaffolding where no one works this afternoon. Turns and steps away. Neither passer-by notices me. My thermos dribbles tea. I hadn't properly screwed on the top. Besides spotting my trousers, splotches gleam on the floor. I plunk my shoulder-satchel down on diamond-shaped tiles to cover the stains. Refreshed, writing in my notebook at a hectic pace, I put it away and step through the wire gate, closing it, as the sign instructs. I'm uncertain if I've left the Madman in His stone House, who waits, with no contradiction, on the path ahead to ambush me with extreme Love.

Find VI: Returning the Band

> In freshening wind the wood edge swells.
> On approach slow-drops ping from sleeves.
> I realise the silky touch that wraps around
> the hair-band's plastic spine, its springiness.
> First, I walk too far in, imagining I found it
> deeper under canopies, so need to turn back
> then remember a marker, the bluebell margins.
> Lowering it to the path, it doesn't seem a child's
> but a goddesses' head-dress. Has she missed it?
> Will I escape from her vigilant guards or be dis-
> membered? Shyly I rest it on twigs and it takes
> the shape of all curved branches on the ground.
> So I leave it there. Wind whirring through trees,
> as through the undergrowth pink campions spy.

The fissured floor starts to re-join; healing-rain
oozes each stiff clod back in place; underfoot
earthy beliefs in wholeness and solidity return.
I don't want to give it up, but have no consent
to keep that labile band. I ask shiny oaks, plain
stitchwort and slender-backed firs for pardon.
They let me stride out through the latch gate.
Just enough light in the sky, to find my way.

Find VII: The Beloved

I ask a scarecrow to speak, if it could, about
the Beloved. It turns its straw head and says:

Beyond what pain is un-understandable
no further torture exists, not burning bars
but the Beloved's arms ready to welcome.
Be confused — who's beloved, who's you.
Can't separate; then accept, be bewildered:
a holy state, the blessedness that follows grief.
The Beloved is already approaching to hold
you between sense and nonsense. Be empty
as my straw legs and head, easily on fire.
Give up on reason, don't fantasise
you can out-smart the Eternal One
or keep your individual pursuits.
The Beloved will use you like a rag
to change the world you now despise.
What's beyond indiscernible sorrow, is Love.
Sniff it when you see the blank wall bloom
and try not to name it — rose or jasmine —
just say YOU over and over to the Beloved.

chiselled dignity —
ears upright — a hare poses —
leaps an earth-bound bird.

I'll let my journey end with the hare among dog violets; though there were once many other observations, ideas and images that accumulated into a hay stack. But these thoughts have slipped from concern, to leave what is written above.

Endings

Appeal to A House Sparrow

for Farrah

Sparrow, Sparrow — they've taken my granddaughter away from me
Quick Little Phillip — they've taken my granddaughter away
In the bare thicket of a hedgerow the rain's trickling down
You chirp away, on your own today, chirruping half the day
My Settled Spuggie — you gone quiet, and now is only rain
Trickling winkling down through the thickset of a hedgerow
Homely Cheeper — I've spent a lifetime or more to you listening
Sailor of the Eaves — if you big ears, tilt your head listen to my plea
If you A Lost Soul Catcher, you biggest wings, bring her safe to me
Bird of Far Arrival — they've taken my granddaughter away from me.

Gaia I

Thunderclap breakers
slip far away from glitter
on the ruffled sand

Limpidly reflected
at the edge — Sanderlings
rapidly in rows

Once they're on the wing —
almost nothing — these footprints —
necklaces on flesh.

Sheep

The flock doesn't mosey into view out of its lowland
towards a silver birch windbreak that rims to the east
the terrain's opening green. Sheep are here, but in
secret, with golden fleeces after a lambing shower.
Somewhere the Beltane lambs butt and pump under
bowlegged ewes — each their stringy tails swinging.
A lambkin leads Mary to school with dancing hooves
or is hung up, after slaughter, headlessly dripping on
to back kitchen straw, a tear in the slaughterer's gaze.
There must be sheep close by nipping ground-weeds or
sheltering by prehistoric mounds when a blizzard drifts
through peaks and lulls — heavy with woolly dreadlocks
each year snipped to new white among heathered stones.
A ram's horn, resonant as a Shofar, calls the pastoral day
to a close for a shepherd with his crook in doubled arms.

The Waiting Room

Unused seats crowd
the lit-up waiting room
bolted against
a stranded traveller.

Along the platform
under notices
latticed benches repeat.

Is it a disembodied breath
rocking the hinged sign?

In the dark flat pit
the double rails
turn to rust.

A slender-bodied
signal light
stands fixated on green
burns into the distance
mocking my late journeys

when youth's loneliness
seemed exhilarating: whole
metropolises flickered by
without one waving hand's
encouragement or welcome.

Where was I going:
to a fragrant lover's bedroom
that night?
who afterwards
fastened her door hard
against imagining travellers.

Did I jemmy open the front lock?

Through the ill-lit house
sneaked, bent over with doubt,
ascending the stairs
tall with hope nudging ajar
the easily swung-open door:

she gleamed, from the window,
in her small corner bed,
as if never aroused
by a human hand.

Small Perfume Bottle

The two-inch tall octagon
reveals the dark auburn fluid inside
nearly gone and yet enough survives
for twenty dabs to beard and hands.

Its dimpled brass cap stays oily.
The old fragrance wearer won't be
distracted by any looming depletion.

He knows his skin or his blessed inhaling,
both too brief miracles, can't confine scent.

Attar, Musk and Oudh — infused rose petals,
deer sac, trees' heartwood — distil visions
only the self's remotest curve can caress.

Yet his fingers sparkle from that excess —
an inkling of paradise before absence.

Holiness has an Address

For Sufi Muhammad Yousaf Sahib

Holiness has a street number in Peterborough.
With an easy knock, a Sufi visited that house.
He had prayed alone years in self-friendship
under His Creator's orders, in another room —
the blue curtains drawn, the furniture sparse —
expectant in hope, forbearing in his failure
to attract not a soul across his welcome mat.
Then some attended, rapped on his own door.
The householder became that Sufi's life-friend.

Today a parade of brothers comes to that address.
Through its narrow doorway, tables stand allied
with floral sheets spread; crispy samosas, onion
bargees, tea and amber strings of candy are served.
The Jaloss, the March, follows the cathedral city's
roads and by-ways twenty-five years have unfurled.
Once, the great Shaykh, staff and gold dome turban,
headed the brothers by ancient and modern thresholds,
past railway platforms where devotees had reclaimed
their belief, in tight rows, angling to the south-east
had stood up, bowed down, prostrated on concrete.
Now, by disused pubs, Arabic scripted lintels, past
where medieval Palmers rallied, the procession
inundates its way round bollards and abrupt kerbs,
it reopens the pilgrim routes to a new destination.

With supple white crowns and exuberant scarves,
the band of marchers progresses down passageways,
between stranded cars at a junction, led by banners
the ivory clothed companions sing out tributes on
Almighty Allah, invoking peace and blessings on

the Prophet Mohammad, His Slave and Messenger.
Grey beards and black trimmed beards, their loose
garments swishing. A green sandaled-ensign waving.

It all began with a Sufi's scented breath, handshakes
and a labour sweetened heart; the man who opened
that door saw holiness in his neighbour's face and
pondered where it came from and who led the way
to the highest virtue, the most humble acceptance
in faith, in love in a new, unfriendly place. He said
in his language from thousands of miles to the east
'Let's set out down these Peterborough streets to see
who will join us, who will feed us, who will praise.'

In Search of Water

By what we pictured as a ruined home
you and I abandoned grown up shoes

barefoot pursued sheep paths through
brittle heather, keeping our balance.

For a time we settled in a grassy doline
below the wind. 'This place... so

beautiful.' I puzzled
at the untouchable 'vibe' you

absorbed. What existed further
below the afternoon vegetation

you listened up-side-down, stretched-
out, legs above your head that sloped

towards the sink's tapering base
before unpinning your headscarf.

Then on, till our ways separated,
we left peat-prints and squelched

through greenest moss-beds for joy
letting liquid ooze between our toes.

Around and overhead on every side
between earth and sky, a repertoire

skylark, curlew and bahhing ewes.
At last my face broke the sun's pool.

I found the source had been cut back
and teetering from a foothold, peered

into a deep gash: in secret, in disbelief
continuous water crept from red rock.

You sat by a crafted, oldest well
now covered by a steel grid.

There, you read the miracle
that came during my absence.

Peace overflowed the gapped wonder
between fell rims and valleys;

at each vantage cobalt and cloud rose
traced by outlines of crumbling walls.

On return, our paired shoes looked
anxious to be re-entered, socks under tongues.

With a sweep you re-fastened your scarf,
my green fleece became our prayer mat.

On a lost people's labour-undulated ground
we made a late, middle-day, prayer of thanks.

A bee zipped past as if on a global flight,
fallen stones shone as if they'd rise again.

Our coats buttoned, we withdrew from the land,
climbing a rickety fence, finding our way back,

with no reason to depart each said to the other
'I could have never come here, but for you.'

Two Cathedrals (of Liverpool)

On this frigid, light-shifting Friday noon,
ahead, at the boulevard's eastern extent,
as if the split-ends of a torn mourning-veil
hail-frayed clouds caress the one Shelter's
pink-grained walls and non-intricate tower.
A slow focusing path weaves up and inside
to a giant-made cavern where the bluest glass
strives to share stonework's unwavering climb.

At the street's other close, countless concrete steps
ascend inelegantly toward an immense circular tent
of ringing sheets. This other Cathedral almost flaps
if steel-pegged against the next unpredicted raiders.
Inside, its altar stone is set at the conical core, with
worlds of space left for a would-be God to shape.

The Shaykh and the Dead Baby

Omar wrapped the baby in a blanket and carried it to the Shaykh's door. Omar was hoping for a miracle; he'd heard that the Shaykh had saved others. An attendant answered. Omar said he wanted to see the Shaykh and have him touch his dead baby. *That's impossible,* said the attendant, *he's grieving the death of his wife and any more grief would be unbearable.* He turned Omar away. Omar started to walk aimlessly. Who knows how long he walked carrying his baby covered in a tender blanket? Omar couldn't go back to his wife. He couldn't face her sorrow and he knew, though he didn't want to, he would blame her for the death. He had to keep walking; there was nothing else to do. No one paid attention to him as he trudged along through busy hot streets, stopping now and then to catch some shade. At least once and probably more, he pulled back the laps of the blanket to stare at his baby again: may be she'd be breathing by now. He looked at her purple mouth and locked eyes, holding her stiffness gently. He closed up the bundle and started to stroll again. A friend saw him and came over and asked, *what are you doing? You can't carry a dead baby around forever you know.* Omar stopped and was polite but unmoved. His friend was disinclined to drive the point home, and quickly left Omar to his perambulations. The mourner walked on through exhaustion and wretchedness. Where was he going? There was nowhere to go. At last he began to think about the Shaykh and his disappointment that the 'great one' couldn't help. He had been his only hope. But gradually Omar considered the master's sorrow and started to feel for his bereavement. He decided to do a Du'a. Finding a secluded place not far from a mosque and placing the baby with great care on to the ground, he began to pray for the Shaykh. Who knows for how long he was on his knees with raised cupped hands? Omar forgot everything else, concentrating more and more, his heart was drawn toward the Teacher's heart. At last Omar came out of his reverie and looked down. To his astonishment his bundle and baby had vanished. He feared a dog might've come along and snatched up his child. But it was unthinkable that he wouldn't have noticed such a thief; or perhaps some local trouble-maker had taken it. But no, he would've surely heard any such disturbance. Of course he also thought that wherever his baby might have gone, it must be alive.

Bruises of Home

to my mum, nearly 96

For the Sensitive Plant has no bright flower;
Radiance and odour are not its dower;
It loves, even like Love, its deep heart is full,
It desires what it has not, the Beautiful!
PERCY BYSSHE SHELLEY

Mum's extreme aging colours the house.
Its decor has altered with her collapsing
into a near eternal absent-minded-ness.
Should I still obey her? It's unreasonable
not to respond and what does it cost me?
I'm her first born, her long remotest son
returned. I bow, kiss her hospital bruises
on the back of her right hand, black-blue
roundish shadows on sensitive plant skin.
Perhaps, her survival, her years, rekindles
a distant but true respect and compassion.
Back home in an elegant back room (60yrs
in the same house her victory) a screen door
opens out on a comfortable spring afternoon.
A mellow sun has migrated all the way round
to glow through the century old, stalwart maple
not yet giving shade to her home's westward face.
A pink-rouge and amber sunset will delight later.
'Hey, don't squeeze me too hard', she complains
as I attempt to raise her up from a favourite chair.
'You'll give me another bruise.' And she does
not need another badge of service to longevity.
And by far has enough black holes in memory
like further emblems of her patient endurance.
'I'm forgetful,' she might insert in a dialogue
of sorts. 'It's been ages since I've seen you'

when I've only stepped out for an afternoon.
Sometimes looking up at four framed photos
she describes them as my wedding pictures
from three decades ago, sometimes as her
grandson's, from three months in the past.
Perhaps, such details hardly matter, when
absence colours her every recollection; she
has too many to remember who've departed
before her to set any event or person in time.
Though her pressure marks on her hands and
arms are naturally understandable to me and
her carers, they continue baffling to her as if
without a source. 'Was I attacked in my sleep?'
She might at once exclaim the query and not
recall an assailant. Who, to accuse, or pardon?
Her pleasure at having me back, at home, after
some years, begins to wobble. Temperate days
of sharing pass but she doesn't gauge or absorb
their accumulation with a prospect of their end.
Either, I have been around for too short a stay
after a long time or too long after a short age.
Her mis-proportioning, so child-like, contains
her existence with no calibrated past or future.
Like looking into a fairy tale book, she engages
moments through limitless tints of reds, greens
blues, blacks, yellows, whites, golds; by these —
not by a measured ticking on wall or her wrist.
I could wish to be a partner in her time-free-ness.
Can such faith engulf fear? She's snapped chains.
An incredibly delicate Prometheus… unbound.
Gradually, for her, years require no boundaries.
And a mere week ago falls off into the infinity
from which she came; each tomorrow can't be
yearned for but slides into an un-emotive zone.
So, she can't retain a grudge or plot a revenge.
A strange mercy accompanies her acute aging

that allows consciousness without being obliged
to pin-point the offence, attack, pleasure or love
with perhaps one dear exception. Those smudges
on cheeks and limbs fade into an afterglow of
purpled tulips, stained roses. Subtly mum fades
too towards a reality of not being here, a quiet
prep for her disappearance into a blaze of light
a final — not-near-death — experience. Or she may
sneak down a colourless hallway; hear from its
lamp-lit staircase, her dead husband's voice call-
ing from 70 years ago, from an attic card table
'Hey, come up! We need ya' for a foursome.'

Stairs in Deep Snow

Each tread could be a lost foothold
and still half-indicate the way below
turned delicate, so tenderly undone
making that going down seem vast.
Who can shed its sense of hope?

Rilke saw an upward climb, beyond
the summit step he praised our arriving
into emptiness. And the Chinese poet
who depicted the well-bucket entwined
with scented flowers, made it immovable
when before it had been easily lowered in.

It is not clear if anyone skips down
closing their eyes to how shape expands
to become shapeless, or tramples beauty
forgetting its silk threads join truth and love.
Not certain that an ancient actor
realises when to step off, if it's possible
to achieve footprints where the wind's formed
a tapering screen across each angled stair.

The aged one defies, keeps maturing against
time, grows wilder and older, older, wilder,
her sight nothing but intimate and strange
her body's a stink, a franticness and aching
as if there could never be one moment to
gaze, study or predict the effects of snow —
descend and accept losing her balance —
but instead with one unavoidable misstep
must slip off the stage, in a second be gone.

Father-Son

We quarrelled on that all but final day
before I meant to leave home for good.
We came to blows. I'd sworn at him.

He couldn't tolerate that from his son.
My mother and sister raised their arms
high, stepped between, shouted our names.

Seeing his Missus and daughter shaking,
with a complete twist of the head, dad
retreated. I heard a series of doors shut

and half-collapsed on the bottom step
of the stairs; my mum squeezed in beside
embraced me, my sister stood over me.

But I kept imagining what my dad was
thinking, down in the basement among
the furnace pipes and his old army rifle.

When I heard his heavy gait return I froze.
Unchallenged he placed a hand on my shoulder
and said, 'It doesn't matter. You're my son.'

Washing your Corpse

I wash across your black and blue forehead
wrinkled; rinse out into a shallow bowl
and pat and stroke with a damp face cloth
your purple nose, inside your ear's whorls
and back around your stubbled chin, over
collapsed cheeks to your brow's under-edge
then ease my flannel round off-colour eyes,
a yellowish moss oozing from these ovals —
is this what tears over a lifetime become?

I'm careful, maybe too careful. I don't want
to damage anything: who knows how easy
it is to puncture a collar bone's slack skin?
I wipe your arms, into the concavities of your
elbows, then the top and bottom of your wrist,
no pulse of course, back up your pitted right arm.
My white gloved hand slides round each finger
across ten old nails like blackened beaches.

I am taking too long, but I can't rush this
labour. I want to un-soil your every location.
Each fibrous dip and rise, each creased opening
and viscid closure — (who knows why?) as if
details have meaning, I'm giving you dignity
down to your feet, bending to a last practicality —
attaching name and age — I fasten with string
a brown label not too tightly to your big toe.

Between Tide-lines

A boy and his young sister and I struggled between
tide-lines on a North Cypriot, out of season, beach; pebbles
and rotund stones and 'skimmers' had been tossed in heaps,
with each step our shoes dug in we gave up half a stride.

We played hide and seek among surf-edged eucalyptus;
with eyes closed, I counted while the two siblings sought
a good hiding place; they crouched behind the boldest trunk
with initials craved high and low in its too fleshy bark.

Neither made it 'home free'. In no time, I spied them.
Light dulled; the foreshore moaned; pebbles were muscled
up the beach then forced back into the next wave's in-rush.
With each blue-turquoise turning a long hissing white

I saw perched, on a sea-ringed boulder, my old Shaykh,
his green turban riffled, his Spring juba buttoned to the chin.
At the core of his world-cuddling love, he sat in seclusion.
I gave distant Salaams and pictured 'an ocean in an ocean'.

Dragon-Butterfly

I watched a Medina butterfly as a dragon,
flame-exhaling, frail as a twilling leaf,
in the Holy Prophet's noonday mosque.
Above scented, packed worshippers
an ochre, crimson-fuselage creature,
wings roaring, flickered high and low

until over first-time and veteran Hajjis —
our smooth or creased foreheads down
and fingers stretched to each mat's fringe —
the airborne contradiction vanished,
only clinging to bright vertical marble
a second more in case I refused to believe.

May I drop my head in that blessed place
again feel prayer's fire through His window.

White Deer In Bradgate Park

For Ayesha-Nur

Among groomed copses on trampled, bracken hills
that unfurl this way and that, with widdershins paths,
the white deer forage under a single tree. Their antlers
rise v-shaped towards a Spring day's prolonged blue
while their heads browse new greens in partial shade.
One, shy, absently, throws a dark-eyed glance at me.

'I'm safe, in this enclave, from your hounding world.
Here with my fellows, for hours we frisk, in innocence
hoof time, feign wounds, or lie prostrate as a Muslim.
My whiteness has incited marvels and love; the humble
on quest, entranced in pursuit, dared torrents and cliffs.
Don't believe, I lack power to startle, if I look subdued.
My heart's weak, ready to break; I can't trot at your side;
if you're kind you might see to whom — each night — I fly.'

Infant Land

Somewhere out of range
giant shoulder hills rest
crystalline in flames of snow,
dark-jade ocean unfurls a tonnage of foam,
naked sandbars cringe; elsewhere freezing fog
glazes two lit-up ships, one bound for port,
the other toward open water.

In an ash bordered field, through
patches of sun, around cut-down trunks
pallid bushes are on fire with green buds.
I follow close my young guide's
lead through hollows
and over broken mounds.
Just outside his walled city,
a newness blooms. A future
rises from the past. Once buried
under wreckage and toxins
guarded saplings burst
outcast earth breathes, befriended.

We soldier on, picking up debris
a burning wind throws against
his infant land.

Red Candle Holder

Our bedroom candle holder's
blackened around its tinny socket;
we've given up chipping off the wax
clinging in layers like paint remnants.
To carry it to our bed the shallow dish
extends an incomplete ring as a handle
not big enough for a man's curled finger
but still too expansive for a child's.

Many mornings we've seen the thing
spent, as a gift that no one can use,
and reeking. But don't close the drapes.
Now it's settled on our white window sill
against blind glass, let it be a reflection
because it can never speak for itself.

To My Granddaughter Farrah

This year I'm the strawberry picker who,
but stiffly, bends and seeks among yellow-
hearted white blooms and under curly leaves
where the plump scarlet drops might be hiding.

That random fruit straddling the garden path
intrigued your appetite. You stooped, craved
until nimble hands searched them out, until
'round your lips and each fingertip was stained.

This estranged season I feel on upturned palms
the burden of that sticky red and must wonder
how this colour that predicts taste of sweetness
gives a sense of all promises drained away.

But, lacking your sharp-strawberry-insight,
I probably miss half their message of love.

Intriguing Farrah

Intriguing Farrah

Granddad your beard tickled
and tufts of snow grass
bounced down the hillside —
among bright green mosses
I tramped in flowery boots.

We came to a stream,
you held my hand in yours,
I leapt across —
then you let me do it myself
I said, *Again, again, again.*

I stepped along stones
then slipped off and fell
Granddad you made me laugh.
I made a fallen wall a train,
I was the driver, *hooting.*

Granddad, are you listening?
I stumbled over snow grass,
pretending, my hat almost fell off.
You smiled and looked to the sky
and I jumped up on my feet.

One wellie wobbled off
then you stooped to help
put my pink sock back inside.
I collected bracken rods and
moss balls; put them in my pocket.

Remember the grazing sheep?
You pointed out, on approach,
how one gazed back toward us
but when we reached the fence
they'd all gone over the hill.

We came to a pointy tree.
I wanted to snap a limb,
you gestured *no, don't...*
You coaxed a branch down
and showed me its capped buds.

Coated, scarved and hatted
we journeyed through pasture
one big big rock to the next;
we took turns standing high
on top each, loving what we saw.

I believed I was a pirate
shuffling along a black plank
when I climbed that fence prop —
under my arms you lifted me off,
like a giant, on to the other side.

Granddaddy I called you,
did you see the gold
glowing around my head
or mistake it for the hill top
behind me sloping to infinity?

You, you eye-reader-teaser
you, you happy bumble 'aphazard-er
you plunker-lunger-'unter-tummer,
then you gave me your answer —
but I had more words coming fast.

You gave me a packet of nuts,
salted and sweet crescents, I liked
them wildly. I asked their names.
Cashews you said so definitely
your back turned facing homeward.

I wanted to twist off
a little stone from a boulder
I shouted *It's stuck!*
I didn't ask you to lift it for me
but you polished it with your sleeve.

Sometimes I couldn't speak.
I looked up and saw your eyes
raised toward chatter chatter.
Your mind was in the clouds
mine was in the clouds too.

You wanted to go through
a gate into higher fields.
I kept pulling you back
towards the steepest slope.
I wanted to drop into that gully.

Those were my favourite jeans.
I went down again and again
till their knees were all dirty.
You never grew grumpy or
tried to brush off that earth.

You stopped and listened
you said, to unseen water moving
through the land. I couldn't hear it.
When you knelt, level with my ears,
I heard its winding sunny shape.

I wasn't frightened
on our long searching.
The big teeth dog didn't frighten me.
I wondered where my fear had gone.
Perhaps it hid under your hat!

Foot-holds down to hand-holds
you tested each for true-ness,
guided me into my gully.
I couldn't climb out. You picked me up.
I liked it when you carried me.

At home you had told me
stories, but I didn't ask
for one where land and sky joined.
I had so much more to say then
words that peeped out.

You didn't think about mud
or whatever, wore only shoes.
Up and down wouldn't be hard.
You tied your laces over and over.
They have to be tight, you said.

There were no flowers
but the after lunch sun
had yellow petals; they made
bracken wands and grass blades shine.
I pulled up some for a gift for everyone.

I want to go to the sheep,
I said; you explained they'd
all disappear over the hill again.
OK, Granddad, I accept, your way.
Kept quiet my endless hope.

I plumped down on
a clump of tender, dry grass.
I stood up and it looked like a seat.
I offered it to you. After a long time
you lowered your bottom into my chair.

I didn't chit-chat or squeal
in that high wall-less room
with Vs of light that you felt.
I couldn't stay in my make-believe
dungeon, crying out, *help! help!*

I left my dolls at home
some big, small, plastic, some tickly
my cuddly creatures from the toy box.
Under the day's blue boulder
you were my companion.

You'd said, *I'm going to the hills*
and I asked if I could come,
you looked really surprised.
How could you not know
that when you leave I miss you?

I had fun tripping over a stump
and on my knees staring up at you.
I wanted to know what you'd do.
You didn't run to my rescue
but grinned at my creating.

Everything was direct
for me, I couldn't name
half of what I saw, unlike you
wiggling brilliant patterns
across each hill's body.

When you drove, I knew
I was a special guest. You stopped
to show me horses feeding.
I couldn't see over the wall
but could feel your sadness.

I wanted to jump
where the water was wide.
You said, *I wouldn't make it.*
I watched the light around
stones chuckling at my dare.

Sometimes my shadow
was bold then it faded
but stayed attached to me.
Sometimes I jumped into yours
to see what happened then.

I didn't think
I could make it through
those rough weeds. But I followed,
lifted my legs and stomped
arriving at where you were.

I saw your car far off,
I wanted to go back home.
You let out, not a word.
I changed my mind
and climbed further.

There was that silence
I didn't tend to know
and no painful dreams.
I heard my own breath
when two hills cuddled.

I showed you a ladybird
stuck on a stick
part of a knobby tree.
She looked too still
as if one of your buds.

I got a little frustrated
trying to say something difficult
from the child seat
my first time on my own
in your box on t' top red car.

My hands poked. I tried
to yank from the ground
an old grey wheel.
Around it the earth popped.
I don't think you heard that.

I imagined what fish swam
with shiny fins unseen
under my stretched legs
when I cried out *Again, again.*
Perhaps someday I'll know.

You held me tight to cross.
It was more than a little way,
my first leap was over an ocean.
I saw something in the waves
I wanted to see it always.

Sometimes I ran like crazy
and I saw my shadow
on a far away slope.
When I stopped, I wondered
why it didn't keep running.

I wasn't the jealous one
I was a rhymer
telling tales, playing the vet,
when the hills turned to
clouds I was ready to step.

I wanted to cover
you in sheep's wool
because you were so funny.
Like your white beard hairs
you twisted and turned.

It was your day
I didn't see the moon
or a cow jump over the moon.
I would've like to, but was happy
with your silly *moo moo*.

Granddad, I didn't find a witch
or hear a mouse squeak
or meet a dog to give a bone
but I saw a wheel in a silver gown
and eyebrows on a chimney.

At first I didn't believe
you were the delicate one —
you much taller, with bigger steps.
But among cool wind and half sun
you needed my smothering.

Our trip to the far hills.
On the way back down
I imagined what I might tell.
I pushed open the door to home
with my fading grass and mosses.

There was pain indoors,
sadness in the hall, up the stairs.
In my bedroom with muddy knees
before someone changed my clothes
I wanted to return to those hills.

Secrets I kept inside.
They spoke in my sleep...
I had to make more of these.
I wasn't sure if enough, I hope
now they're enough to give you peace.

The bright sacred ones were
all around on that high hills' day.
They moved the water this way that
and helped the sun across the sky.
They join us now though we're apart.

I was always teasing you.
Why why why I hear you puzzle.
Because I love you, Granddad.
And here's my poem book
my little gift to you.

If we stayed there
all night under the stars
would the sky's arms hold us?
Of all I know, I don't...
I know our day was real.

When you read
these words that you can
that I can't, remember
the hooting of a stone train,
my shaking snow-grass.

Lightning Source UK Ltd.
Milton Keynes UK
UKHW011811060320
359913UK00003B/180